The Handbook of Biblical Psychology:

Tools for Overcoming

Dr. Mark S. Majors

The Handbook of Biblical Psychology: Tools for Overcoming
By Dr. Mark S. Majors

Printing Year 2011

Copyright © 2003, 2004, 2005, 2006, 2007, 2008 & 2011 Handbook Press: Branford, FL

Most Scripture quotations are from the King James Version (KJV), and are KJV unless otherwise noted: New International Version (NIV), © 1973, 1978, 1984, International Bible Society. of Zondervan Bible Publishers; God's Word (GW) is a copyrighted work of God's Word to the Nations Bible Society, © 1995; New King James Version (NKJV), © 1982, Thomas Nelson, Inc.; The Holy Bible, English Standard Version® (ESV®) Copyright © 2001 by Crossway, of Good News Publishers.

All rights reserved. No portion of this publication may be reproduced, distributed, stored in a retrieval system, or transmitted in any form or by any means, including electronic, mechanical, photocopying, recording, or otherwise, unless otherwise stated within the document or without the prior written permission of the publisher, except in the case of brief quotations embodied in critical reviews and certain other noncommercial uses permitted by copyright law.

Published by Handbook Press

PRINTED IN THE UNITED STATES OF AMERICA

Cover/Book Design: Mary J. Majors, Handbook Press.

International Standard Book Number: 978-0-9821249-2-5

Contents

Preface   v

Part I: Foundations to Biblical Psychology   5
Chapters
1. Introduction to Biblical Psychology   6
2. Made in the Image of God: Our Construction   13
3. The Fall of Man and Our Sinful State   19

Part II: The Bible's Presentation of Psychological Structures   25
Chapters
4. Thoughts; Our Mental Activity   27
5. The Mind: The Point of Control   35
6. The Heart: Our Moral Nature   43
7. Made in the Image of God: Fully Conscious, Fully Aware   51
8. Nurture: The Impact of the Family on Our Psychology   55

Part III: Godly Understanding of our Earthly Experiences   59
The Psycho-Emotional States of:
- Anger   61
- Love   65
- Hate   67
- Humility   69
- Pride   71
- Peace   73

States of Mind:
- Depressive   77
- Depression II: Detailed intervention strategies   81
- Anxious   85
- Anxious II: Interventions in Anxiety states   89
- Addictive   93

Appendix A   Intimacy Intervention for Marriage Relationships   95
Appendix B   Scriptures on Marriage/Family and Church   99
Appendix C   Scriptures on the Heart from Proverbs   103
Appendix D   Scriptures on the Heart from Psalms   105
Appendix E   Scriptures on Freedom   109

Dedicated to my Lord and Savior Jesus Christ, for it is His Word that is contained within, and His Will that brought this work into being.

Loving thanks to my wife Mary J Majors, whose loving care, encouragement, and edits made this work possible.

A warm thanks to many pastors for their encouragement, edits and theological advice.

My appreciation to and blessings to the many students who endured the early forms of this work with editorial comments, joy and thanksgiving.

Preface

I went through a secular psychology program to earn my Ph.D. in counseling psychology. During that painful process I often wondered why God would call me to learn so much material that was inconsistent with His Word. A few years after completing my academic work, God began to wake me night after night in the early morning hours to read in Genesis. After a few months of repeatedly reading from Genesis chapter one, the reason for the long secular education became clear to me. God wanted me to write about His psychology of man as articulated in His Word, and the foundation of that psychology is in the book of Genesis. The Ph.D. work gave me the information necessary to separate out the secular from the Biblical.

There is no need for outside resources for studying the psychology of man. God explains it all very clearly in His Word. Unfortunately, this is not an attitude that is held in many Christian colleges and seminaries today. This text is intended to provide the truth of man's psychology as given by God to allow schools and universities to return to a purely Biblical foundation for ministry and education. This work is not exhaustive, but is intended to be a foundation upon which diligent study of God's Word can transform lives within the discipleship and counseling process.

PART I:
FOUNDATIONS OF BIBLICAL PSYCHOLOGY

Chapter 1:

INTRODUCTION TO BIBLICAL PSYCHOLOGY

Psychology is the science of behavior and the mental processes that underlie all forms of behavior. In contrast "Biblical" Psychology is not a science! It is however, a study of God's Word presented in the Bible. The term psychology is from the Greek word *psyche* meaning soul, and the Latin/Greek word *logy* meaning the discussion of, or word (today it is rendered the study of, or science of). The term soul is the non-physical nature of man, or principal elements of mental and spiritual life: the thinking, willing nature. It is not the spirit of man yet it involves the spirit. It includes the emotional responses, but they are interconnected to the mind and thus need not be treated as a separate issue. Therefore, a definition of Biblical Psychology is:

> The study of the thinking and
> willing nature of man as
> expressed and described by
> God, the creator of man, in the
> Holy Bible.

God has not left us to wonder about our nature. He has given us a complete description of our thinking and willing nature, which provides an understanding for all of our behaviors and experiences during this life. Knowing our Biblical Psychology provides insights into our relationships with God and fellow man. It is the foundation for discipleship and providing Biblically sound counsel to the Body of Christ. Our Biblical Psychology is our psychology, and there are many lies and distortions that have been presented by man that result in undermining our knowledge and understanding of the truth.

The Lie

As the secular science of psychology emerged over the last few centuries, Christians stopped looking to God for information about their psychological nature and embraced elements of the "science." Unfortunately the term "science of psychology" is mostly false and a lie that enslaves individuals to man's thinking. The "science of psychology" is dominated by the central philosophy of the antichrist (man exalted above God) - not a science at all. One of the few areas of secular psychology and medical science that is worthy of **cautious** study is physiological psychology (neurological science). This branch of psychology tends to be a presentation of what God has created. Yet, even this area is contaminated with notions from atheism, and the reliance upon Darwin-like evolutionary explanations of what is seen. Non-Biblical philosophies in science are philosophies, not science. They represent desperate efforts on the part of foolish men and women, who say in their heart that there is no God (Psalm 14:1), to find understanding to their short and futile lives. Their unspiritual minds are puffed up and blinded, unable to see the truth.

Many who read this text will be shocked at the completeness of God's explanations of our psychology. This is a result of the belief that the Bible is not sufficient to guide (we need man more than God) when it comes to the psychology of man. Today in most seminaries and Christian colleges an introduction to psychology is provided by one of many standard secular texts, or other texts that are dominated by secular thinking. The mistaken assumption that secular psychology is a science has led many individuals to embrace it as a fact. It has therefore become a commonly held view in the Body of believers that secular counseling and the "science" of secular psychology have much to offer. Further, this line of thought leads students to the conclusion that God has left the important work of our mental health to the wisdom of man. This is not a belief that is presented in this work.

Every effort has been made in the preparation of material for this text to remove all of the contamination of secular psychology that has made its way into contemporary Christian thinking. Scriptures are presented as foundations for the explanations and examples that are provided. Any overlap with secular psychology is solely due to the fact that once in a while man will figure something out correctly (when inspired by God). At meaningful locations in this text some of the various major trends in secular psychology are presented in a text box or insert for the purpose of understanding the influence of some of the more dominant worldly distortions on our thinking. This is provided for contrast and understanding, not education.

The Bible is the inerrant Word of God our creator, and it is lacking nothing.

> *All Scripture is given by inspiration of God, and is profitable for doctrine, for reproof, for correction, for instruction in righteousness: that the man of God may be perfect, throughly furnished unto all good works.*
> (2 Timothy 3:16-17 KJV)

If we believe that discipleship, teaching, and giving counsel are "good work," then what we need is contained in the Bible. We simply need to look.

Biblical counsel and discipleship

Frequently Christians forget that the world is a battleground where there is a war that is raging between good and evil, truth and deception. There is only one standard for truth, and that is the Word of God. This text uses the Bible to provide a psychological foundation for all Christians who are called into ministry, and all Christians are called (Matt. 28:19). Regardless of the specific ministry area of study (pastoral, counseling, Christian education, missions, theological or others), knowledge of how God has created our psychology is critical to the understanding of the self and others. The Word of God as illuminated by the Holy Spirit is to be the foundation of our lives. At the core of the beliefs for this text are the sufficiency of Jesus Christ (the living Word) and the power of His indwelling Holy Spirit. All born again believers are given that Spirit.

> *Ye are of God, little children, and have overcome them: because greater is he that is in you, than he that is in the world.*
> (1 John 4:4 KJV)

Frequently Christians forget that the world is a battleground where there is a war that is raging between good and evil, truth and deception.

The great commission presented at the end of the book of Matthew tells us that we are to make disciples of all nations. The process of making a disciple of Jesus Christ requires that we teach them God's Word. We are to provide sound Biblically based counsel that aids in the growth and development of the Christians in our lives. All of us need to have people in our lives that provide us with discipleship training and Godly counsel. The study of Biblical psychology provides an understanding and accurate interpretation of the experiences that are common to us all. Those common experiences are often the topic of counsel and encouragement. The truth of God's Word sets us free from the bondage of misconception and lies that are perpetuated by the world and satan. In this text the term Biblical counseling indicates a process of intensive discipleship that focuses on one or more areas of needed growth. The act of providing Biblical counsel is the same as providing discipleship training, but it does tend to be targeted toward a more narrowly focused set of issues.

It is important to evaluate the scope of providing counsel within the body of believers as described in the Word of God in order to understand the breadth of its implications for our lives and ministries. We are all called to minister the love of Jesus Christ to one another. The result of loving others with the love of Christ is that we learn about ourselves. We learn to accept others as they are, just as Christ accepts us (Rom. 15:5-7). We are told in Proverbs (11:14) that the wise individual has many counselors. But where does the role of the Biblical counselor fit into the church today? Is Biblical counseling a profession or an occupation? (see the text box; *"Who is to provide counseling within the Church?"*). Providing counsel to others can be considered to be an element of the duties of pastors, teachers, evangelists, prophets and all positions of authority (e.g. elders or deacons) prescribed in the Word of God. Some people believe that counseling falls solely under the responsibility of the pastor.

> ### Who is to provide counseling within the Church?
>
> In the Bible we find that counsel is provided by the Lord (I Kings 22:5), given to one another (II Chronicles 22:5), and provided by prophets (II Chronicles 25:16). In Proverbs 15:22 we see that plans fail for lack of counsel and success is based on the counsel of many. In Isaiah 11:2 the Holy Spirit is referred to as the Spirit of Counsel. Counsel is said to come from the wise in Jeremiah 18:8, and Jeremiah himself gives counsel (38:15). Jeremiah 49:7 indicates that the prudent have counsel and Ezekiel 7:26 that counsel is given from the elders. In I Timothy 5:14 Paul indicates that he gives counsel to younger widows. King David had counselors (Ahitophel, II Samuel 15:12). In I Chronicles 26:14 Zechariah is referred to as a wise counselor. In 27:32 David's uncle, Jonathan, is described as a counselor, a man of insight. It is the name given to Jesus Christ in Isaiah 9:6, given to the Holy Spirit in John 14:26, 15:26 and 16:7.
>
> **In Sum**, the Bible indicates that Godly counsel is provided by Godly individuals within the Body of Christ. One can argue that providing Godly counsel requires an extensive and in-depth knowledge of the Word of God and a maturity in faith and life that lends itself to understanding, compassion and acceptance. It is hard to fathom that an individual can be called to pastor a church without that calling including the element of counseling. Part of the role of this text is to provide the missing pieces from the education of pastors who believe that they are poorly equipped to fulfill the obligation of counseling in their pastoral calling. It is also intended for the purpose of equipping **all** those in ministries that involve giving Godly counsel to others. This includes all Christians for all are called to ministry.

Yet many, if not most, pastors today believe that they are ill equipped or not adequately gifted to provide this form of care to members of their congregation. Typically this line of thought on the part of the pastor has been formed through their learned belief that counseling requires some measure of extra Biblical education or special gifting. These beliefs are largely a result of secular psychology's assault upon seminaries, Christian universities and the minds of all believers. The world says that the Bible is lacking in provision for our mental health. Too many Christians believe the lie and embrace the false teaching that leads to pain and suffering. It is the lack of "Truth" (Bible) that causes the pain and suffering in the world today.

When we think of Biblical counseling as being discipleship then the distinction between leaders and all believers disappears. All believers are called to make disciples. Therefore to some extent all believers are called to provide Biblical counsel. There is however a difference based upon calling. Those who are called to ministerial positions of authority in the Church will tend to be the ones who more consistently deal with the more intensive personal and interpersonal issues. This text will not be concerned with the distinction of calling, and is intended to be a foundation for all.

Secular vs. Biblical counsel

Fundamental to the deceptive beliefs found in secular psychology is that we are born without flaws and the world around us makes victims of us all. The Bible teaches us that our sin nature entered into our human race at Adam's fall – we are all born with it. While the evil in the world should be uncomfortable to the Christian's regenerated sensibilities, we are victorious in Christ Jesus, not a victim. Because of the erroneous secular belief that we are born without sin, counseling (and even much of Christian counseling) focuses on understanding the victimization (damage to our purity) and gaining power through a life of heightened self-focus (frequently referred to as enlightenment). It is unfortunate that these beliefs have permeated the fabric of our Christian culture because they are in complete opposition to the Word of God and they make freedom from the sin that so easily entangles us impossible.

Within the Christian culture today, it is widely believed, and frequently preached on Sunday mornings, that dealing with the issues of the day requires something more than Jesus Christ and God's inerrant Word. In contrast, the Biblical view of providing counsel is the systematic presentation of Scriptures, which provide the understanding and power necessary to be helpful to all. To give counsel requires a Biblically based understanding of the occurrence and presentation of symptoms, syndromes, and patterns of behavior that are the manifestation of the effect of the sin nature of man and/or the impact of this fallen world on our lives. Yes, we are at times the victims of our own and others' inherited sin, but only Jesus Christ can save us from ourselves, not the secular psychologist. We are more than conquerors though Him.

Overview of Text divisions:

This text is divided into three main parts. It is not an exhaustive look at what the Bible says about our psychology, for that would take a Bible sized text. It is an introduction into thinking about ourselves as God thinks about us.

<u>Section one</u> focuses upon how we are created and the fall of man. Being made in God's image means that we are perfectly made. Yet, the contamination of our sin nature has stained God's perfect creative work. Knowing information about God's attributes help us understand our own. The damage caused by sin and death is the principal problem that affects our psychological health.

<u>Section two</u> of this text presents the structural component parts of God's psychology of man. The interaction of our thoughts, mind/soul, heart, emotions and behaviors are clearly presented to us in God's Word. This discussion of our psychology is critical for those who provide counsel. It will reveal how secular psychology opposes the truth in God's Biblical psychology. Chapter 8 looks at the importance of how the family impacts psychology development.

<u>Section four</u> deals with specific personal issues that are common to us all. Issues involving depression, anger, anxiety, and hate as well as love, joy and peace are presented in their Biblical context. This information is not exhaustive, yet it provides a clear indication of how completely God has given us a psychological handbook, the Bible.

Throughout this text you will find inserts referred to as:

TOOLS FOR OVERCOMING

These tools will be given within the text body and in informative boxes (tool boxes) that are inserted to provide practical discipling and counseling tools and tips. These tools represent knowledge from God's Word that is to be used in everyday life and ministry. The truth does set us free. God's truth is plainly given to us in His Word. Satan and the world have provided the Christian with all manner of contamination intended to pull us away from the love of God. Secular psychology attempts to help or save us by leaving us in the hands of counselors of pseudo-science and deception. The truth is that the world's help is demonic and destructive. Under the disguise of education and enlightenment evil has spread like the yeast problems that Jesus referred to as plaguing the Pharisees. True wisdom and knowledge come only from God. The Bible tells us that we perish for lack of knowledge of the Word (Hosea 4:6). As this text is read, the reader is encouraged to note how often they have heard the psychology of the Bible spoken against in Christian literature, workshops, and sermons. Notice how clearly God's answers for our psychological issues are presented.

The information in this text will change your interactions with others as God's Word changes you. Spend time reflecting as you learn the truth of God's gift of our psychology. Put what you learn into practice. God has given us the ***Tools for Overcoming;*** it is up to us to use them.

Father in Heaven,
We pray that You would, by the power of Your Spirit, open the eyes of our hearts to clearly see You and know Your Word.
In Jesus' Name.
Amen.

Chapter 2:

MADE IN THE IMAGE OF GOD
OUR CONSTRUCTION

Let us make man in our image, in our likeness... Genesis 1:26

Knowledge of the truth about our construction starts in the creation story that is found in the Bible. In Genesis 1:26 God said "Let Us make man in our image." We know from the Bible that the image of the living God has three fundamental parts: Father, Son and Holy Spirit. This is what the "our image" in the passage relates to. It is not stated in the singular "my image," but in the plural "our." Throughout the four Gospels Jesus describes the unity of the Father and the Son,

I and my Father are one.
(John 10:30 KJV)

Believe me that I am in the Father, and the Father in me... (John 14:11a KJV)

And the union of the Father, Jesus, and the Holy Spirit is clearly presented at the moment that Jesus was baptized.

And the Holy Ghost descended in a bodily shape like a dove upon him, and a voice came from heaven which said, "Thou art my beloved Son; in thee I am well pleased.
(Luke 3:22 KJV)

Because we are made in the image of the triune God, we have three similar corresponding parts to ourselves, and yet they are each one individual. The table below describes the separate components of man and their interrelationship with the three parts of God.

Component parts of God and man

God	Main Attribute	Man
Father	Controlling Will	Soul
Son	Physical earthly Form	Body
Holy Spirit	Life-giving supernatural	Spirit

The Father

In the Bible, God the Father is described as possessing the will (Mt. 12:50), knowledge (Mt. 6:8), and causality (Col. 1:12; Eph. 1:3). He thinks, chooses and causes things to happen in the universe and in our life. In computing terms the Father is the Supreme, Supernatural Central Processing Unit. God the Father relates to our human mind or soul (Mt. 11:29, Lk. 1:46; 2:35, Act. 14:2, 22). The soul is typically described as being composed of the mind, will and emotions (see discussion on the soul below). With our mind, we think about and make the choices in our lives. We cause things to happen by our thoughts and will. We choose good or evil with our mind. God only chooses good.

The Son

Jesus experienced in His body all of the sensations and emotions that we have (Heb. 4:15). He is the true physical manifestation of God in the flesh (John 1:14). He is representative of our physical bodies. Because of Christ's true human existence, we can be comforted by the fact God understands all of the trials that we may experience as our bodies send messages to our brain about its cravings and wants (our fleshly demands). Jesus truly knows of these experiences and our physical sufferings. The pain He experienced upon the cross, the rejection felt from His own family, the grief expressed while weeping for Lazarus, and many other documented experiences demonstrate that He was man in the flesh.

The Spirit

The Holy Spirit of God represents the dynamic supernatural, life-giving power of the trinity.

> *But if the Spirit of him that raised up Jesus from the dead dwell in you. . .* (Romans 8:11a KJV)

The Father's will is manifested in the powerful actions of the Holy Spirit.

> *Not by might, nor by power, but by my spirit, saith the Lord of hosts.* (Zechariah 4:6b KJV)

The Mind; the Soul; the Spirit??

In this text we will use the term Mind, not the term Soul, to avoid the confusion that often occurs in separating the terms Soul and Spirit (Heb. 4:12). Soul is often found to be "*nephesh*; breath, soul, self" coming from a root that means "that which breathes," and consequently has a body, or simply "a breathing body." Therefore, it is different than the mind (νους, *noús*, διάνοια, *diánoia*, σύνεσις, *súnesis*): No precision is found in the terms used for mind: The Old Testament and New Testament lack anything like scientific precision in the use of terms that indicate mental operations. The English language had few such terms until the late 1800s.

In the Old Testament *lebh* is made to stand for the various manifestations of our intellectual and emotional nature. We are often misled by the different renderings in the different versions, both early and late. Sometimes *nephesh* or "soul" is translated "mind" (Deu 18:6 the King James Version, "desire of his soul" or "mind"); sometimes *ru^{a}h* ("spirit") is translated mind (Gen 26:35, "grief of mind," *ru^{a}h*). Sometimes *lebh* is used, as in Isa 46:8, "bring it to mind" (literally, "heart"), or in Psa 31:12, "I am forgotten as a dead man out of mind" (literally, "heart"), as in Septuagint, *kardía*, and in Vulgate, *a corde*, Luther, *im Herzen*, new Dutch translated, *uit de gedachtenis* (i.e. "memory").

In the New Testament the words *nous* and *dianoia* are used, but not with any precision or consistency of meaning. The Epistles of Paul provide the most clarity for use of these terms. They are used sometimes in connection with (sinful) flesh as in Col 2:18, "puffed up by his fleshly mind," sometimes in direct contrast to it, as in Rom 7:25, 'with my mind I serve the law of God; with the flesh the law of sin.' In Titus 1:15 it is brought into a parallel understanding with conscience ("Their mind and their conscience are defiled"). Phrases like "a reprobate mind," "corrupted in mind" occur elsewhere (Rom 1:28; 1Ti 6:5). From this state of "reprobation" and "corruption" man must be saved. Hence, the necessity of complete transformation and renewal of the inner man (Rom 12:2), "transformed by the renewing of your mind (*nous*)."

To avoid the mistranslations and thinking that arise from the term soul, the word mind will be used where it is known to be correct based on today's understanding of Hebrew and Greek.

The function of our spirit is the life force within us.

> *He bowed his head, and gave up his ghost (spirit).*
> (John 19:30b KJV)

We have a fundamental spiritual nature that can be in communion with God's Spirit if we know Jesus Christ and choose to listen. The Holy Spirit is referred to as the Counselor, Comforter, and Guide, and the act of Christian counseling can truly be thought of as a spiritual process. He is the Spirit of Truth that leads us into all truth.

Three in One

The three elements of man are separate components of the whole of man, just as the triune God is One God.

> *And the very God of peace sanctify you wholly; and I pray God your whole spirit and soul and body be preserved blameless unto the coming of our Lord Jesus Christ.*
> (1 Thessalonians 5:23 KJV)

There is a need for our spirit, mind and body to function in harmony just as the Father, Son and Holy Spirit function as one. This beautiful balance of the three components given to us by our Creator requires constant mental, physical and Holy Spirit maintenance. Whenever one of our three components begins to malfunction, a destructive cascade of the whole person is possible if the condition is left untreated (Pv. 17:22).

TOOLS FOR OVERCOMING

A Counseling/Discipleship Point

As an example of the variation in form by which a psychological problem can present itself, consider the following brief discussion about depression. An individual with major depression who is contemplating suicide has lost much of their mental clarity (**mind**), stops taking care of their **body**, and their **spirit** longs for death. This is the result of a total cascade breakdown of the whole person. As we will explore in more depth in the third section of this text, depression can begin in any of the three component aspects of man. For Example:

- Physical injury or illness that is life threatening or protracted (occurring over a long time period) in nature will often result in depression (usually mild). This is very common for those who have had a heart attack or cancer.
- Long-term (chronic) or short-term (acute) physical, sexual or emotional trauma (abuse) and stress has an impact on the mind that can lead to depression. This is particularly possible if there is little or no personal support. It wears down the neurological functioning of the mind.
- Lastly, our culture is currently full of spiritual depravity that causes hopelessness and despair. The result is that there are record levels of depression and suicide.

Therefore, an important aspect of providing good counsel and discipleship in the Body of Christ is discerning which component (body, mind, or spirit) is most appropriate to be the initial focus of helping. It can provide a fundamental answer to the question "Where does it hurt?" All of the situations and events that have occurred in an individual's life that have led up to the presenting situation cannot be undone. It is important to take the most effective action possible. The power of discernment comes from learned Biblical wisdom and listening to the Holy Spirit's leading.

If any of you lack wisdom, let him ask of God, that giveth to all men liberally, and upbraideth not; and it shall be given him; (James 1:5 KJV)

But strong meat belongeth to them that are of full age, even those who by reason of use have their senses exercised to discern both good and evil. (Hebrews 5:14 KJV)

Knowing the proper place to intervene is just the first step. The questions of how and when to make the intervention are other concerns to be thought and prayed through.

The Lie

The world believes that we began our journey into man's current form starting from rainwater falling on rocks. The world believes that man was not created and that there is no creator at all. Over millions of years man has slowly evolved from a few strands of amino acids through various animals stages to reach his current condition. Because of this thinking, insights into the psychology of man are believed to be achievable by the study of monkeys, rats and pigeons. This Darwinian focus has created damage to the psychology of man, yet it is the foundation of modern secular psychology.

The Bible tells us that if we give into, and are dominated by our flesh, then we exhibit uncontrollable beast like behavior. The secular psychologist and humanistic thinking want us to believe that our psychology is animal in nature. The world wants us to think that it is normal, healthy and natural to act like the other animals since we came from the same source and are thus cousins.

Many secular psychologists state that our lusts and desires are not to be denied. Sexual perversions are explained as natural responses to desires and should not be blocked. The lie of satan is that we are animals and should spend our lives in self-exalting pride, covetous lust of the eyes and constantly feeding our flesh. When an individual believes the Darwinian humanistic teaching, then satan's message makes good sense.

The evolution lie denies God and the truth of creation. It enslaves people in sin and death. Jesus came to set us free from sin and death. We are made in God's image. The only relationship that we have with the animals is that we have the same creator. Only we children of God are made in His triune image.

Understanding Suffering

Suffering is the pain that brings a person to the point where they believe that they need to seek help and counsel. It is a disruption on our psychological or mental health and daily lives. It is motivating.

There is no shortage of suffering in this world (Matt. 4:24). It takes on many forms and has many causes. The scourge of cancer and heart disease are both common assaults on the physical body. Depression and Schizophrenia can be chemical imbalances in the mind. Separation from God and willful sinning leave the spirit sick and desperate. Demon oppression and possession are like the actions of muggers hiding in the dark to do injury and harm. Each of these issues is a result of the sinful world in which we live. From the moment of the fall of man (third chapter of Genesis, and the focus of the third chapter of this text) there has been suffering (Rom. 8:22, 23). This will be the case until the return of our Lord and Savior Jesus Christ. We must take and give comfort in the truth that He has overcome all of the suffering (John 16:33). Jesus is our answer.

Suffering:

One of the most destructive myths in the Christian community is that suffering will not occur in your life unless you have sinned. As a result of this belief members of congregations will not talk about their problems until things get so bad that something catastrophic has or is about to happen. One element of this destructive belief will manifest itself in the false happy face found on many believers every Sunday morning. At the other extreme are the persistent whiners who quickly wear out their welcome in any conversation. The correct attitude is found in James, who says that we are to "Consider it pure joy, my brothers, whenever you face trials of many kinds." Note that it does not say if we face trials, but when we face trials. As Christians we are not to go it alone. The Bible says that we are to bear one another's burdens (Gal. 6:2), and strengthen each other by our testimony (Rev. 12:11). If we are all so full of pride that we cannot confide in each other, we offer nothing to the world that it does not already have, PRIDE. We will suffer the rejection from the world as Christians (the sufferings of Jesus). This may be the most painful of all sufferings, but we are to accept one another in the Body of Christ as Jesus has accepted us.

Chapter 3:

THE FALL OF MAN AND OUR SINFULL STATE

Pre Fall Man

Without an adequate foundation all work eventually crumbles. Genesis is the foundation of our belief in God. It is also the foundation of our understanding of sin, suffering, and the general fallen nature of the world in which we live. Before the fall there was no suffering and no need for counselors. God made man for fellowship with Him. God made Woman (Eve) for fellowship with Adam. The time that Adam and Eve spent in the garden was a time of fellowship and peace. No bad weather or storms ever came up. In fact there was no rain (Gen. 2:5). There is no mention of death or dying, disease or illness, damage or rot. God was present; He enjoyed walking through the garden in the cool of the day (Gen. 3:8). There was no form of separation between God and man. Man had no knowledge of good and evil. He had a direct relationship with the Creator, and knowledge of Him. In God's image man was sinless and pure.

The psychology of man during the time in the garden must have been similar to that of God's psychology. The similarity was in form not quality. Man was not constructed to die, and thus his psychology was not designed to relate to that experience. Before the fall we can only think that Adam and Eve had a perfect and healthy psychology. If we take the statements about being made in God's image seriously, then no problems or breakdowns could have occurred in man's psychological nature. No stress, no strain could have occurred in the daily garden life. No fear or anxiety could have existed in the lives of Adam and Eve because the true love of God cast out all fear (1John 14:18). Man had control of the mind, control of the emotions and control of the body in which he lived. Adam was given a job, a wife and great place to live and work. He saw the face of God. He had it all! We can only imagine what it must have been like, but then Adam sinned and became separated from God.

The Fall

Was there evil in the garden? Yes, we know that the serpent (satan) was there, therefore evil was there. This may be shocking to some that think that this would go against the perfection that existed in the Garden of Eden. We know that satan was cast out of heaven along with the other rebellious beings, and fell to earth (Lk 10:18). Evil existed in the garden and had no effect over anything (no power), until Adam and Eve made a very bad decision.

> ^{1}*Now the serpent was more subtil than any beast of the field which the LORD God had made. And he said unto the woman, Yea, hath God said, Ye shall not eat of every tree of the garden?* ^{2}*And the woman said unto the serpent, We may eat of the fruit of the trees of the garden:* ^{3}*But of the fruit of the tree which is in the midst of the garden, God hath said, Ye shall not eat of it, neither shall ye touch it, lest ye die.* ^{4}*And the serpent said unto the woman, Ye shall not surely die:* ^{5}*For God doth know that in the day ye eat thereof, then your eyes shall be opened, and ye shall be as gods, knowing good and evil.* ^{6}*And when the woman saw that the tree was good for food, and that it was pleasant to the eyes, and a tree to be desired to make one wise, she took of the fruit thereof, and did eat, and gave also unto her husband with her; and he did eat.* ^{7}*And the eyes of them both were opened, and they knew that they were naked; and they sewed fig leaves together, and made*

themselves aprons. ⁸And they heard the voice of the LORD God walking in the garden in the cool of the day: and Adam and his wife hid themselves from the presence of the LORD God amongst the trees of the garden. ⁹And the LORD God called unto Adam, and said unto him, Where art thou? ¹⁰And he said, I heard thy voice in the garden, and I was afraid, because I was naked; and I hid myself. ¹¹And he said, Who told thee that thou wast naked? Hast thou eaten of the tree, whereof I commanded thee that thou shouldest not eat? ¹²And the man said, The woman whom thou gavest to be with me, she gave me of the tree, and I did eat. ¹³And the LORD God said unto the woman, What is this that thou hast done? And the woman said, The serpent beguiled me, and I did eat.
(Genesis 3:1-13 KJV)

What was Adam thinking? He had it all, why eat the fruit? Let us examine the account of the fall one step at a time. Why did Eve eat the fruit? In verse six we read that she saw that it was good for food, pleasing to the eye, and desirable for gaining wisdom. How was she deceived by satan? She said to satan that she was told that if she ate the fruit from that tree she would die, but satan said in verse four "You will not surely die." Let us try to understand all of the mental transactions (thinking) that took place in Eve.

First, the deceptive words from satan affected Eve's mind so that her thinking about God's spoken word was changed. She became convinced that there would be no punishment if she ate some of the fruit. This was a lie that Eve was open to receive. Once there was the removal of punishment, then Eve thought that she could do what she wanted to do. Eve lost her fear of God, and without the fear of God her wisdom vanished. In the Bible we see that the fear of the Lord is the beginning of wisdom, and knowledge of the Holy One is the development of understanding (Pv. 9:10). The fact that God had told her (or Adam) that she was not to touch that tree or eat its fruit did not matter to her anymore. With fear of punishment gone, the birth of disobedience came.

Eve knew God in a closer more personal way than anyone of us knows Him today; walking and talking with Him; truly sitting at the knee of the Father with nothing but peace and joy in heart and mind. Yet we see that she turned from the perfect love of God, and even lost that healthy fear with the wisdom that goes with it, at the suggestion that you can do what you want without punishment. This style of thinking represents the first control issue of man, rejection of God's authority. God was in control and had set the simple boundaries for Adam and Eve. The possibility that she would be like God if she ate the fruit may have been enticing enough in itself to cause Eve to disobey. Given the sin nature that we see in all of us today, it is possible that it was Eve's desire to reject God's authority and be in control herself that prompted her behavior. There is some indication that she stopped long enough to think about what she was doing, but a discussion of her thoughts reveals that her thinking had become flawed and did not help her in this situation.

Second, the fruit was seen by Eve as good for food. Her stomach must have growled at the appearance of this food. With no Godly wisdom her stomach began to increase in the prominence of her thinking and to rule in the mind (carnality). She did not need to eat that particular fruit. God had made every type of good and pleasing fruits and nuts available from the trees in the garden for their consumption. This was not a case of limited choices or deprivation. It was the sight of seeing something good to eat, but in reality was not good for her; that was the problem. Today we have sugar and many processed foods all of which are wonderful to the taste, but result in all types of problems (diabetes, obesity and hyperactivity to name a few). The problem for Eve was that this fruit looked good to eat, but she was told not to, and that it would kill her. How common today for individuals to see something that looks good and, knowing that it is bad for them, to eat it. The undisciplined enjoyment of comfort foods and the satisfaction of the taste buds and stomach are indications that the body is controlling the thoughts in the mind. This represents a loss of control over the body's cravings.

Third, the fruit was pleasing to the eye. Eve wanted to have what had not been hers (covetousness).

Seeing and wanting drives our American culture. We have learned to want what we see and at the same time not be able to discern our needs. Individuals go into great debt (slavery) to have what they see others have. Eve wanted what she did not have and mentally deceived herself into thinking she should have it. It cost her very life to get it. A two-year-old in a shopping cart will quickly reach for anything interesting on the grocery store's shelf that is within reach. Even after being told no, the child at the first opportunity (when mom is not looking and punishment may not occur) will reach and grab. The child has no control over his or her wants. To see it… is to get it. Eve's thinking had driven God out of her heart. To fill the emptiness, stuff must be had. Without God in the heart of man the lust for what we do not have surfaces in what can be described as an out of control desperation. This is another control issue that takes on the form of "Know God and control lust, No God and lust controls you."

TOOLS FOR OVERCOMING

The Genesis Example

Because our sin nature is tied up so completely with the Genesis fall, it will be helpful to examine the sin behavior of those to whom we are ministering in comparison to that of Adam and Eve's. By asking a series of questions based on Genesis, we can often quickly understand what the root cause of their behavior is.

1. How did they delude themselves into thinking that there were no consequences for their sinful actions?
2. What elements of the natural man (biological/carnal) have taken control over the decisions that are being made?
3. Have they lost control over their wants, and seem to never stop pursuing material interest or wealth?
4. In what ways have they traded the truth of God's Word for worldly wisdom?
5. How are they attempting to shift responsibility to the devil, spirits, or other individuals?
6. Do they present themselves as victims of others' behaviors, circumstances or God's will?

Knowing what fundamental sin thinking is involved in the person's motivations and actions, allows the counselor to direct them to a Godly prescription of confession and repentance.

<u>Fourth,</u> satan told her that "you will be like God, knowing good and evil," and she saw that it was desirable for gaining wisdom. She had true wisdom before this moment. There is no indication anywhere in Genesis before this point in time that she lacked anything. Having decided that she did not need to fear the Lord she was in search of another form of wisdom. Worldly wisdom tells us that we are naked. It tells us to rate, rank and evaluate ourselves based on others. She did not want to be Adam's helper any more; she wanted to be his boss. To be like God was to be in charge. To have knowledge is to be in

control, and to have power. The act of seeking worldly knowledge and wisdom can represent an effort to build ourselves up. It is pride working in our mind. This is not to be confused with the education that helps us in our careers or to gain employment (yet for some this can become a problem). Eve had a job… a good one. She was not simply trying to better herself. Did Eve want to be better than God? We know that she wanted to be at least equal to God. Eve wanted to be like God and was seeking to increase her pride (this thinking caused satan to be thrown out of heaven). This is self-esteem, not God esteem.

Sin Entered Through Adam

With all of this attention on Eve one might want to make her responsible, and that's exactly what Adam attempted to do (Gen 3:12). But, she was the helper and Adam was her supervisor. Sin entered through Adam, not Eve. He was responsible for everything he allowed to happen. He was right there with Eve and listened to everything that occurred. He was the one given the instructions, don't eat it! He made all of the same decisions and mistakes in thinking that Eve made. If his love for and fear of God had been intact, he would have walked away, or grabbed her arm as she was reaching for the fruit. Why did he fail to speak up when she even approached the tree? Why do Christians fail to speak up when we observe other believers reach for sin? Adam simply took the fruit and ate it. What was he thinking? He was not thinking. Adam wanted the same control, power and status that Eve wanted and she ate the fruit and she did not die. Adam must have thought that God was lying and the serpent knew the truth. He convinced himself to not believe God. This is the first case of someone following a worldly individual and turning his back on God. Eve was deceived. Adam ate the fruit without deception, but with deceit (he hid).

After the fall: The Onset of Sufferings

What happened next was the first incidence of discomfort and suffering. Both Adam and Eve had their eyes open and knew that they were naked. God's glory had left them and they were naked and uncovered (this glory condition may have been similar to the condition of Jesus in Luke 9:29). They did not like that uncovered state, and worked to cover themselves up by sewing fig leaves together. They were enslaved by their bodies and for the first time man had to go to work to get clothing. The rubbing of the fig leaves on their virgin skin must have caused the first rash and sores. We do not know how long they wore the leaves before they were found out, but it would not have taken very long to begin to cause discomfort and pain. What a shock to go in an instant from clothed in God's glory to seeing naked bodies; from light to darkness. They had to cover up the sin.

The Bible tells us that they hid from God when He came to walk in the garden. Was this to avoid punishment, or the first act that represents man's belief that he can hide himself or his sin from God? It is very common to provide counsel with someone who has been involved in a sin behavior for a very long time; they talk and act as if they believe that no one knows what they have been doing. Or perhaps, they do not really believe in God. Either way, until the sin causes them serious distress, they do not come in for counseling. Often when they do finally come in the response is similar to Adam's response to God when He asked him "Have you eaten from the tree that I commanded you not to eat from?" Adam's response is an attempt to blame both God "The woman you put here with me," and Eve "she gave me some fruit from the tree and I ate it." This pattern of thinking on Adam's part is consistent with the way the world responds today. He pronounced his victimization (the woman you put here) and avoided his responsibility (she gave me some) for taking and eating the fruit.

When discipling or providing counsel to couples who are experiencing relationship challenges this pattern of thought is often pervasive in both husband and wife. He will exclaim that he calls her names because she "stupidly" spends all of their money. She states that she spends all of the money because she feels bad about herself when "he calls me names," and subsequently shopping helps her to feel good about herself. This all means "I am not responsible for what I choose to do…. you are." Individuals actually believe that they are off the hook with respect to the sin that they commit, by virtue of the sin that others commit. The insanity of this line of thinking represents two forms of control issues.

> *It is irrelevant where the sinful notions come from. Our response to sinful thoughts in all forms from any origin is to be the complete rejection of them.*

<u>First</u>, it proclaims that another has control over my behavior.

<u>Second</u>, I am not in control of myself, or "I am a victim of your behavior."

Eve blamed the snake. It was the first time that the defense "the devil made me do it" was used. An interpretation of Eve's statements and behavior is that she believed that she was not responsible for her sinful thinking and desires. The deception presented by the serpent should have had no effect on Eve's obedience to God regardless of life or death. Even if eating the fruit would not result in dying, the command not to eat it was in effect.

Today it is all too common in Christianity to hear of behavior and choices based on sinful, prideful desires that are blamed on spirits or satan. It is irrelevant where the sinful notions come from. Our response to sinful thoughts in all forms from any origin is to be the complete rejection of them.

Adam and Eve's attempts at avoiding responsibility did not work. Sin cannot be hidden from an all-knowing all-seeing God. We all suffer in this earthly life for our own, and Adam and Eve's bad choices. But, if we are alive in Christ, then the consequence of death for our sin is nothing more than a brief transition moment leading to an eternity of life with a loving God.

Eve ate the fruit and offered it to Adam. They both listened to the words of the world/satan and not those of God. Adam and Eve wanted to be the same as God. Their sin resulted in the fall of man and subsequently all of creation. These are the simple facts, but the results are widespread and permeating. As a Biblical counselor, every suffering individual that is seen for counseling comes as a result of the fall of Adam and Eve. The punishment for the behavior that Adam and Eve chose is death, toil in procuring food, struggle in authority and suffering in childbirth.

> ^{16}*Unto the woman he said, I will greatly multiply thy sorrow and thy conception; in sorrow thou shalt bring forth children; and thy desire shall be to thy husband, and he shall rule over thee.* ^{17}*And unto Adam he said, Because thou hast hearkened unto the voice of thy wife, and hast eaten of the tree, of which I commanded thee, saying, Thou shalt not eat of it: cursed is the ground for thy sake; in sorrow shalt thou eat of it all the days of thy life;* ^{18}*Thorns also and thistles shall it bring forth to thee; and thou shalt eat the herb of the field;* ^{19}*In the sweat of thy face shalt thou eat bread, till thou return unto the ground; for out of it wast thou taken: for dust thou art, and unto dust shalt thou return.*
> (Genesis 3:16-19 KJV)

Things are not right on earth because of the fall. The very nature of man and the whole of earth is flawed because of the original and continuing sin. In Isaiah 24 we read that the earth is defiled by its people, and that a curse consumes the earth. In Romans 8:20-22 Paul talks about the earth's bondage to decay. The result of the fall is more than the specific suffering prescribed by God to Adam and Eve. It is all of the suffering and pain that we have today. If the suffering is from a behavior that was sinful, someone did it, and people suffered because of it. If the suffering is from disease, sickness or death, they were all unleashed by sin (in Christ Jesus we have overcome these). Flaws permeate nature as a result of sin. The psychology of man is stricken with all types of problems and shortcomings.

When individuals ask, "why has God allowed this to happen to me?" the answer is that this (whatever it is) was not part of God's perfect plan. Death comes from the fall and sin. Sickness and disease result because of the ravages of satan. When someone has died, often a suffering person will remark "God could have stopped it." This is true, but He did not cause it, and many times He does intervene and stop evil. In fact through Jesus the Father has given us power over all of the works of satan (Luke 10:19). The problem is that there exists a common belief today that we are to be free from suffering if we pay our tithes and are kind to folks.

> *The result of the fall is more than the specific suffering prescribed by God to Adam and Eve. It is all of the suffering and pain that we have today.*

This is nonsense. Suffering is part of the fallen world in which we live. Man's free will that allows him to choose to love his Creator is the same free will that allows him to choose evil, and hurt others. To cancel free will is to change reality so that we are no longer made in the image of God. Our God has a free will that is constrained only by his perfect and good character. If we choose to take on the character of His Son Jesus, then we will also have a constrained free will. We give our free will to God, or we give it to satan.

There is no suffering apart from the fall and no salvation from the suffering apart from Jesus. Suffering is at times not the result of the suffering individual's sin choices, but it is nevertheless the result of someone's sin, or the flawed natural world of which we are a part.

As God was sending them out of the garden, He killed some animals to provide a skin covering for Adam and Eve. Blood was shed to cover sin nature. This was the first sacrifice to cover sin. The old covenant provided for the use of the blood of animals to be presented as an atoning sacrifice. In the new covenant Jesus gave His Blood to cleanse us all. In this way we that accept Jesus as Lord and Savior can stand in front of the Father in Heaven clothed with the righteousness of Christ, and free from all sin.

Frequently individuals will point to the fact that Adam and Eve did not die a physical death at the moment they ate the forbidden fruit. They did die a spiritual death, and they knew it. It took about 900 years for the sin to kill Adam. He did not die a natural death, as there are no natural deaths (man was not constructed to die). Death comes because of sin ("The wages of sin is death;" Romans 6:23). Man was not created to die and death will never be acceptable to him. Yet, the sting of death is gone, through Jesus we live forever.

The lie discussed in previous chapters, that we are born perfect and then damaged by our environments, is completely wrong. Adam and Eve were perfect. The choice to sin has infected every individual. Cleansed by the Blood of Christ we are again perfect in God's sight. Therefore the truth is that we are born flawed and made perfect through Christ Jesus our Lord and Savior. Belief in the lie means that you don't need a savior. The psychology of the world leads man to the second and eternal death.

To fully understand the damage to the psychology of man that resulted from the fall it is necessary to have a grasp of the basics of the structural elements of man's psychological nature. The next sections of text will present the structure and the later chapters will discuss more specifics of the fallen psychology.

PART II:
THE BIBLE'S PRESENTATION OF PSYCHOLOGICAL STRUCTURES

In this section of the text God's presentation of our psychological construction will be examined. Previously we studied that we are made in the image of the triune God. Our components of mind, body and spirit correspond to the Father, Son and Holy Spirit. The focus of this section will be upon the activities of the Mind and its interactions with the outer environment and inner psychological world. Just as all actions of the Godhead are under the authority and control of the Father, the actions of man are under the authority or control of the mind of man. The Bible refers to the thoughts, mind, heart, spirit and body/flesh as interacting together to form the everyday psychological functioning of man. Being in ministry requires that there be a deep understanding of these interactions and God's rules for a healthy mental life. Further, to provide wise counsel about life, knowledge of our psychology needs to be at hand. The Bible gives it all.

The world today is contaminated by secular psychological theories. Many of the individuals that we minister to will be stuck in their suffering due to beliefs that are the product of secular psychology's lies and influence on the Christian culture. Throughout this section of the text there will appear textboxes that briefly present the major theories that influence the beliefs about man's psychology today. All of them will in some degree be in opposition to the Word of God. All of them have influenced most of the Christian world to some extent and being able to identify them is very important. As mentioned previously the secular world sees man as being a victim of the experiences that they have. It believes that all of our mistakes and suffering are from being exposed to external stimuli that impacts our lives and "causes" the mistakes and suffering. This is in opposition to the Bible's clear statement that it is the fallen world and our sin nature that "causes" all of our problems.

God has given us a complete set of instructions to understand, correct, and maintain our mental health. These instructions are typically not found with "Christian Psychologists," which are often Christians that are practicing some form of secular psychology. This section of text is the presentation of God's Word on how we are constructed mentally (including some aspects of man's emotions). While the spirit of man influences his psychology it is not a part of the mind, and for that reason will not be included directly in the discussion. Psychology means the study of the soul. Our use of the term soul is the "whole of man," similar to the phrase "the number of souls lost in a shipwreck." Some refer to the soul as the mind, will and emotions. Some add to that the intellect. A good way of conceptualizing this material is that it represents a Biblical understanding of how we know and are known by others in our lives.

> ...to provide wise counsel about life, knowledge of our psychology needs to be at hand. The Bible gives it all.

Chapter four will focus upon the thoughts and thinking of man. Our thoughts represent the activity we all experience as our internal speech, sounds, and pictures of life. Thoughts are internal products of our mind, heart, and spirit or from other external influence.

Chapter five gives understanding of the mind and its control and filtering function. The mind is controllable with the help of Christ Jesus. Knowledge of its operation helps us gain clarity in understanding many of the issues we face today.

Chapter six presents God's description of the heart of man. This core element of our psychology has moral foundations regarding our behavioral patterns.

Chapter seven reveals how being fully conscious, fully aware is the likeness of our Creator God. Our free will is a blessing, yet causes much pain and trouble.

Chapter eight provides a brief overview of the family's impact upon the health and development of our psychology.

Our behavior, emotions and motivations will all be presented throughout these chapters as constructed and chosen expressions of these functional parts of man.

Our Creator has made us with great complexity. We can experience a strong sense of peace when we understand our psychological nature as a wonderful gift from God. We are made in His image and nothing is lacking when we are In Him.

Chapter 4: THOUGHTS: OUR MENTAL ACTIVITY

"For as he thinketh in his heart, so is he..."
(Proverbs 23:7a KJV)

Many of us have heard the statement by the French philosopher René Descartes (1596-1650) who said "I think, therefore I am." This is just a re-enunciation of God's Word in Proverb 23:7 which states that our thoughts are how we are known. This mental activity of thinking, or the production of thoughts, occurs continuously within our mind. As we study what God has said about our thoughts, keep in mind the truth that we are made in His image. We think because God thinks. Yet our thoughts are not like His. We are made in the image of God, yet not with the same quality of thoughts as God.

> *"For my thoughts are not your thoughts, neither are your ways my ways," saith the LORD. "For as the heavens are higher than the earth, so are my ways higher than your ways, and my thoughts than your thoughts."*
> (Isaiah 55:8-9 KJV)

> *How precious also are thy thoughts unto me, O God! how great is the sum of them!*
> (Psalm 139:17 KJV)

> *O LORD, how great are your works! And thy thoughts are very deep.*
> (Psalm 92:5 KJV)

Even though we have the mental process of thinking, it is clear that our thoughts are not in any way the same as God's. The purity and complexity of God's thinking process is immeasurably greater than ours. Later in this chapter we will see the effect of the fall on our thinking and thoughts. God's thoughts are Holy, while our thinking tends to be corrupted by the fall and our sin nature.

Another way that we differ from God with respect to the thinking processes is that He knows our thoughts:

> *Thou knowest my downsitting and mine uprising, thou understandeth my thoughts afar off.*
> (Psalm 139:2 KJV)

> *He hath shewed strength with his arm; he hath scattered the proud in the imagination (thoughts) of their hearts.* (Luke 1:51 KJV)

> *And Jesus knew their thoughts, and said unto them, Every kingdom divided against itself is brought to desolation...*
> (Matthew 12:25a (KJV)

> *And Jesus knowing their thoughts, Jesus said, Wherefore think ye evil in your hearts?*
> (Matthew 9:4 KJV)

> *But God hath revealed them unto us by his Spirit: for the Spirit searcheth all things, yea, the deep things of God. For <u>what man knoweth</u> the things (thoughts) of a man, save the spirit of man which is in him? Even so the things (thoughts) of God knoweth no man, but the Spirit of God.*
> (1 Corinthians 2:10-11 KJV)

He knows our thoughts and we only know His, if and when He chooses to give some thoughts to us.

Turn you at my reproof: behold, I will pour out my spirit unto you, I will make known my words (thoughts) unto you.
(Proverbs 1:23 KJV)

For, lo, he that formeth the mountains, and createth the wind, and declareth unto man what is his thought, that maketh the morning darkness, and treadeth upon the high places of the earth. The Lord, The God of hosts, is his name.
(Amos 4:13 KJV)

In the Proverb above the Lord makes it clear that being obedient and humble can result in us being blessed with the gift of His thoughts. Responding to a rebuke requires that we be listening to God, knowing His voice, recognizing our mistakes, and doing what is required of us. More will be said about this in the later chapters on sin and repentance.

As stated above, thoughts are our mental activity. But, where does this mental activity come from? Austrian psychiatrist Sigmund Freud (1856-1939) would say that most of our thoughts are generated by our unconscious mind (see textbox). By examining the occurrences of thought and thinking terms in the Bible, it becomes clear that Freud's beliefs on thoughts are in stark opposition to God's Word on the matter. Thoughts come from seven different sources. It is imperative that all Christians understand these seven sources and learn how to recognize them.

> Thoughts come from seven different sources. It is imperative that all Christians understand these seven sources and learn how to recognize them

Sigmund Freud on Thought

Freud was responsible for making the notion of the unconscious mind popular. The conscious mind is what you are aware of at any particular moment, your present perceptions, memories, thoughts, fantasies, or feelings. Working closely with the conscious mind is what Freud called the preconscious mind, or anything that can be easily made conscious. This includes memories you are not at the moment thinking about but can readily bring to mind. The largest part of the mind is by far the unconscious mind. It includes all the things that are not easily available to awareness. These things included many behavioral elements that have their origins there in the unconscious, such as our drives or instincts and things that are put there because we can't bear to look at them, such as the memories and emotions associated with trauma. According to Freud the unconscious is the source of our motivations whether they be simple desires for food or sex, neurotic compulsions, or the motives of an artist or scientist. And yet, Freud says that we are often driven to deny or resist becoming conscious of these motives and they are often available to us only in disguised form.

This is not consistent with the Bible. There is no mention of the unconscious mind in the Bible. We have no thoughts that we cannot take captive to the obedience of Jesus Christ. Freud would have us to be victims of our unconscious minds. He calls cravings of the body drives that we can't control. Freud is responsible for much of the confusion inside and outside of the Christian church today. Most seminary textbooks on counseling use Freud's terminology and concepts and not those found in the Bible.

First, our thoughts come from our body or five senses. Any sensory information that comes into our brain from one of the five senses can trigger an immediate thought reaction. These senses of sight, sound, touch, taste, and smell are all hard-wired into our brain. When information from the sense organ enters our brain we have thoughts about it. We identify and attempt to understand the information. These attempts at identification and understanding are thoughts. Most of the thoughts triggered by sensory stimulation are simply a response to normal life experiences. The smell of good food, or the cool breeze blowing across your skin on a hot day will trigger thoughts and memories with more thoughts. There are times when our senses take in unclean information and we need to control our thoughts because they may lead to trouble. Seeing a pornographic image requires an immediate decision to look and think about the image or turn away. The decision is a process of the mind (next chapter) and the thoughts can be controlled.

Second, thoughts arise out of the recall of the memories that are stored in our brains. Memories can be brought into our minds by way of a number of triggering experiences. They can be triggered by thoughts, complex thinking processes, sensory stimuli or other events can trigger memories. Many images and sounds in daily life can trigger a stored memory to surface. Memory retrieval can occur with the slightest stimulation by a similar currently occurring experience. At times memories will simply seem to come into our thinking. Memories that enter our minds will initiate thoughts about the memories. Consequently, if the memories are negative the thoughts may also be negative, and conversely positive memories can result in positive thoughts. We may have little control over the triggering of memories (unless we live in an isolation chamber), but we can choose which ones to think about. This control affects the impact that past memories can have on our lives. The term intrusive memory implies that one or more memories persistently arises to cause mental/emotional discomfort and are viewed as difficult to control or stop. With prayer and persistence all thoughts can be placed under our control.

Third, our mind during its normal problem solving and reflecting process generates tremendous amounts of new thoughts. Thoughts are a by-product of the mind's functioning. Sometimes the thoughts that it generates are not godly. We are to be careful what we choose to continue to think about. Repetitive thinking or obsessive thought about anxiety provoking issues can result in an individual being trapped by their thoughts.

Fourth, the Bible refers to thoughts as coming from our heart or the core of our personality (chapter 6). A thought from our heart can give us great insight into our motivations and attitudes. All thoughts are processed in the mind and thoughts from the heart often can dominate the thought processing in the mind. Thoughts from the heart need to be examined carefully with intent to uncover their intent, origin and function.

Fifth, our own spirit speaks thoughts and information into our mind. As part of being made in the image of God, our spirit is an experiential part of who we are. Notions and impressions in the spirit emerge as thoughts in the mind. These thoughts need to be considered and understood. As a child of God we may be frequently warned of trouble through our spirit. The spirit of man is able to receive from all other spiritual powers. All thoughts from our spirit must be checked with God's Word to establish their validity.

> *Sinful thoughts are satan's way of interrupting our Godly activities. If you did not generate the evil thought, do not own it, it is not yours.*

Sixth, the Holy Spirit of God speaks into our minds and hearts all of the time, although, there is often a problem with listening or discerning God's voice. God's most common way of speaking to us is by way of spirit. His Spirit will speak to our spirit or directly into our minds in the form of verbal thoughts. These guiding notions will only become concrete for us if we recognize the origin of the thoughts that are generated by the Holy Spirit. If we know Jesus, then we will recognize His voice.

Seventh, thoughts can be placed into our mind by satan and evil spirits or demons. The question of whose voice we are hearing and the thoughts that are triggered must be understood and dealt with appropriately. The small voices of the demon world can result in confusing thoughts to individuals who are not properly discipled into Christian living and Godly understanding. You may be having a great day in the Lord, walking along singing spiritual songs and without any known reason at all have an evil thought pop into your mind. Satan does not like our singing to God. Sinful thoughts are satan's way of interrupting our Godly activities. If you did not generate the evil thought, do not own it, it is not yours. If an unclean thought is not your thought, then reject it and the one from whom it has come.

How and from where the thoughts originate is important. These seven sources of thoughts all have one thing in common; the thoughts that are generated can be taken captive in our mind. The Bible says that we have control over our thoughts:

> *Casting down imaginations, and every high thing that exalteth itself against the knowledge of God, and bringing into captivity every thought <u>(take captive every thought)</u> to the obedience of Christ.*
> (2 Corinthians 10:5 KJV)

> *And I turned myself <u>(turned my thoughts)</u> to behold wisdom, and madness, and folly...*
> (Ecclesiastes 2:12a KJV)

> *Let the wicked <u>forsake his way, and the unrighteous man his thoughts</u>: and let him return unto the LORD, and he will have mercy upon him; and to our God, for he will abundantly pardon.* (Isaiah 55:7 KJV)

Not only do we have control over our thoughts, but also we are responsible for them. Controlling our thinking allows us to control our behavior and the responses we make in life. Most of the problems that are of a persistent or compulsive nature that we find in our or others' lives will be from a lack of control of thinking. Repetitive sin is rooted in repetitive uncontrolled thinking. As we see in God's Word we are to **"take captive every thought"** and **"make it** (the thought) **obedient to Christ."** The Word of God is our standard for every thought that we have. All evil in our mind can be removed through the power of the Living Word and indwelling Spirit of God.

Choosing to entertain the evil thought is sin. We sin in thought, word and deed. All sin starts with a thought.

Thought and Thinking Scriptures:

The following selected scriptures are presented to give foundation to some of the statements made in this chapter and also to provide an overview of other elements of God's perspective of human thinking and thoughts:

Where are thoughts found (location)? In the mind/heart.

> *But Peter said unto him: Thy money perish with thee, because thou hast thought that the gift of God may be purchased with money. Thou hast neither part nor lot in this matte: for thy heart is not right in the sight of God. Repent therefore of this thy wickedness, and pray God, if perhaps the <u>thought of thine heart</u> may be forgiven thee. For I perceive that thou art in the gall of bitterness, and in the bond of iniquity.* (Acts 8:20-23 KJV)

> *Not only do we have control over our thoughts, but also we are responsible for them*

There are a number of different styles of thinking that are depicted in the Bible. The presence of these styles may help us to understand the nature of the difficulties that are present in an individual's life.

Childish thinking:

> *When I was a child, I spake as a child, I understood as a child, I thought as a child,: but when I became a man, I put away childish things.* (1 Corinthians 13:11 KJV)

Distress and troubled thoughts:

> *Hitherto is the end of the matter. As for me Daniel, <u>my cognitions (thinking) much troubled me</u>, and my countenance changed in me: but I kept the matter in my heart.*
> (Daniel 7:28 KJV)

Therefore do my <u>thoughts</u> cause me to answer, and for this I make haste.
(Job 20:2 KJV)

How shall I take counsel in my soul (<u>wrestle with my thoughts</u>), having sorrow in my heart daily?
(Psalm 13:2a KJV)

Give ear to my prayer, O God; and hide not thyself from my supplication. Attend unto me, and hear me: I mourn in my complaint, and make a noise (<u>my thoughts trouble me</u>);Because of the voice of the enemy, because of the oppression of the wicked: for they cast iniquity upon me, and in wrath they hate me.
(Psalm 55:1-3 KJV)

Our thoughts are known by God:

And thou, Solomon, my son, know thou the God of thy father, and serve him with a perfect heart and with a willing mind: for the LORD searcheth all hearts, and <u>understandeth all of the imaginations of the thoughts</u>. . .
(1 Chronicles 28:9a KJV)

Yet you know me, O LORD; you see me and <u>test my thoughts</u> about you.
(Jeremiah 12:3a NIV)

He hath shewed strength with his arm; he hath scattered the proud in the imagination (<u>thoughts</u>) of their hearts. (Luke 1:51 KJV)

Behold, this child is set for the fall and rising again of many in Israel; and for a sign which shall be spoken against; (Yea, a sword shall pierce through thy own soul also,) that the <u>thoughts of many hearts may be revealed</u>.
(Luke 2:34b-35 KJV)

Search me, O God, and know my heart: try me and <u>know my thoughts:</u> . . . (Psalm 139:23 KJV)

The LORD knoweth <u>the thoughts of man</u>, that they are vanity.
(Psalm 94:11 KJV)

The Bible clearly describes the connection between sin and the thoughts of man.

For out <u>of the heart proceed evil thoughts</u>, murders, adulteries, fornications, thefts, false witness, blasphemies. (Matthew 15:19 KJV)

For from within, <u>out of the heart of men, proceed evil thoughts,</u> adulteries, fornications, murders, thefts, covetousness, wickedness, deceit, lasciviousness, an evil eye, blasphemy, pride, foolishness: All these evil things come from within and defile the man.
(Mark 7:21-23 KJV)

And you hath he quickened, who were dead in trespasses and sins; Wherein in time past ye walked according to the course of this world, according to the prince of the power of the air, the spirit that now worketh in the children of disobedience: Among whom also we all had our conversation in times past in the lusts of our flesh, fulfilling the desires of the flesh and of the mind (<u>thoughts</u>): and were by nature the children of wrath, even as others.
(Ephesians 2:1-3 KJV)

Thus saith the LORD GOD; It shall also come to pass, that at the same time shall <u>things come into thy mind, and thou shalt think an evil thought.</u>
(Ezekiel 38:10 KJV)

The God saw that the wickedness of man was great in the earth, and that every <u>imagination of the thoughts of</u>

his heart was only evil continually.
(Genesis 6:5 KJV)

Their feet run to evil, and they make haste to shed innocent blood: their thoughts are thoughts of iniquity. . .
(Isaiah 59:7a KJV)

O Jerusalem, wash thine heart from wickedness, that thou mayest be saved. How long shall thy vain thoughts lodge within thee?
(Jeremiah 4:14 KJV)

The thoughts of the wicked are an abomination to the LORD, but the words of the pure are pleasant words. (Proverbs 15:26 KJV)

The wicked, through the pride of his countenance, will not seek after God: God is not in all his thoughts.
(Psalm 10:4 KJV)

We are told in God's Word where the focus of our thoughts is to be.

Therefore, holy brethren, partakers of the heavenly calling, consider (focus your thoughts on) the Apostle and High Priest of our profession, Christ Jesus.
(Hebrews 3:1 KJV)

Our thoughts and thinking is to be done carefully. Too frequently individuals do not take their thought life seriously.

From this day on, from this twenty-fourth day of the ninth month, give careful thought to the day when the foundation of the LORD's temple was laid. Give careful thought: Is there yet any seed left in the barn? Until now, the vine and the fig tree, the pomegranate and the olive tree have not borne fruit.
(Haggai 2:18-19 NIV)

TOOLS FOR OVERCOMING

A Counseling/Discipleship Application

The thoughts that occur in our minds and the minds of those to whom we are providing counsel and discipleship are the key for understanding what issues will need to be addressed. Reoccurring memories that result in depressed mood can be controlled by controlling the thoughts that a person chooses to have about those memories. Even though the memory will always be in the storage of the mind if the event associated with it occurred after the individual was old enough, it is a choice to choose to examine and replay the memory in its entirety over and over again. We can choose to stop our thinking process by taking the thoughts captive. This means that we say "NO!" to repeatedly rethinking a memory. This seems simple, yet it is an effective strategy for stopping the thoughts. As seen from the scriptures, we do have control over our thoughts.

All sin comes by way of thoughts that are not properly examined and held to the standard of the Bible. When individuals begin to use the "Devil made me do it" defense for why they have chosen a sin behavior that is ruining their lives, we must gently help them recognize the thoughts and thinking patterns that resulted in sin taking root in them.

All healthy Christians who are actively in the ministry of the Great Commission (this should be us all) are a threat to the kingdom of darkness. There is no shortage of testimony from Godly men and women, who are active in the advancement of the Kingdom of God, telling of the attacks upon their minds by way of evil or distorted thoughts. Our level of activity for the sake of the Gospel of Christ is proportionate to the level of attack on our thoughts. The good news is that we have overcome him (satan) through the Blood of the Lamb and the word of our testimony. If we resist the thoughts and satan, he and his thoughts must flee.

In Sum

> *Our thoughts are where the battle is fought every day of our lives.*

All behavior, speech, and feelings come from thoughts that we have. Controlling our thoughts and taking authority over them in Jesus' name is the way to control our lives. Thoughts precede all of our actions. Thoughts are the key to changing our lives.

Our thoughts are where the battle is fought every day of our lives. We have a responsibility to be vigilant and not allow this inner life to get out of control and result in out of control behavior. The next chapter discusses the mind, which is where the decisions to control thinking are made.

Chapter 5:

THE MIND: THE POINT OF CONTROL

Thou wilt keep him in perfect peace, whose mind is stayed on thee: because he trusteth in thee. (Isaiah 26:3 KJV)

This chapter is extremely important for developing an understanding of how God has structured our mental abilities. The mind of man is the evaluating, experiencing, and decision-making element of our brain. Much of our memories and intellect are stored in the mind. Being made in the image of God implies that both man and God have similar minds. As with the thoughts, the similarity of minds does not imply that they are identical.

God is not a man, that he should lie, or a son of man, that he should <u>change his mind</u>.
(Numbers 23:19a ESV)

Also the Glory of Israel will not lie or <u>change His mind</u>; for He is not a man that He should change His mind.
(I Samuel 15:29 NASB)

Who hath directed the Spirit (mind) of the LORD, or being his counselor hath taught him?
(Isaiah 40:13 KJV)

The Bible gives us a picture of God's mind indicating that it is stable and powerful beyond our comprehension. Man will change his mind but the Lord is the same yesterday, today and forever. Both the complexity and stability are the clearly distinguishing factors between our minds and that of our Creator.

God knows our mind (can examine it) and has control over (can alter it) what happens in our mind. Yet we must remember that He never takes away our free will. When we choose to love or obey Him, reject Him or rebel, it is always done with our free will.

When we choose to make Jesus Christ Lord of our life we are choosing to give our will to Him. When we reject Jesus, we are giving our will to satan.

God will use our mind to help us gain understanding. The scriptural examples below of how God uses our mind to get His point across are very revealing:

The LORD will strike you with madness and blindness and <u>confusion of mind</u>.
(Deuteronomy 28:28 ESV)

There the LORD will give you an anxious mind, eyes weary with longing, and a despairing heart.
(Deuteronomy 28:65b NIV)

The afflictions that God put into the minds of the children of Israel frequently resulted in repentance and eventually restoration.

God knows and rewards our mental activity. After the fall, Adam and Eve did not remember that God could see into their minds. They hid from God and lied to Him, as if He would not know and see what they were thinking. Often when counseling with individuals troubled with a sin behavior in his or her life, we hear them speak as though they believe that God does not know what is going on in their minds. It is as if they believe that they are hiding their minds from God.

> When we choose to make Jesus Christ Lord of our life we are choosing to give our will to Him. When we reject Jesus, we are giving our will to satan.

Prove me, O LORD, and try me, <u>test my heart and my mind</u>.
(Psalm 26:2 ESV)

But, O LORD of hosts, that judgest righteously, that triest the reins (mind) and the heart. (Jeremiah 11:20a KJV)

I the LORD search the heart, I try the reins (mind), even to give every man according to his ways, and according to the fruit of his doings.
(Jeremiah 17:10 KJV)

And the Spirit of the LORD fell upon me, and said unto me, Speak; Thus saith the LOR; Thus have ye said O house of Israel: for <u>I know the things that come into your mind, every one of them.</u>
(Ezekiel 11:5 KJV)

Also in Judah the hand of God was on the people to <u>give them unity of mind</u> to carry out what the king and his officials had ordered, following the word of the LORD.
(2 Chronicles 30:12 NIV)

Man can control his mind just as God can control His. We need God to make this possible, and our fallen nature fights against our controlling efforts. The Bible tells us that we can change the focus or turn our minds. We can seek what God has in mind for us, or we can seek evil. It is this ability to control our mind that makes us responsible for all of our thoughts and actions.

I applied mine heart (mind) to know, and to search, and to seek out wisdom, and the reason of things, and to know the wickedness of folly, even of foolishness and madness:
(Ecclesiastes 7:25 KJV)

All this have I seen, and <u>applied my heart (mind)</u> unto every work that is done under the sun.
(Ecclesiastes 8:9a KJV)

When I <u>applied mine heart (mind)</u> to know wisdom, and to see the business that is done upon the earth: (for also there is that neither day nor night seeth sleep with his eyes:) Then I beheld all the work of God, that a man cannot find out the work that is done under the sun: because though a man labour to seek it out, yet he shall not find it; yea farther; though a wise man think to know it, yet shall he not be able to find it.
(Ecclesiastes 8:16-17 KJV)

Remember this, and shew yourselves men: <u>bring it again to mind</u>, O ye transgressors.
(Isaiah 46:8 KJV)

<u>Settle it therefore in your hearts (mind)</u>, not to meditate before what ye shall answer: For I will give you a mouth and wisdom, which all your adversaries shall not be able to gainsay nor resist.
(Luke 21:14-15 KJV)

Therefore let us not pass judgment on one another any longer, but rather decide <u>(make up your mind)</u> never to put a stumbling block or hindrance in the way of a brother.
(Romans 14:13 ESV)

What is it then? I will pray with the spirit, and I will <u>pray with the understanding (mind)</u> also: I will sing with the spirit, and I will <u>sing with the understanding (mind)</u> also.
(1 Corinthians 14:15 KJV)

> The question that we must ask ... is "who is in control of your mind?"

The question that we must ask (ourselves, and the individuals to which we are giving counsel and discipling) is "who is in control of your mind?" It is a choice of the mind to give the Holy Spirit of God the control and it is a choice of the mind to give the control to the desires of the flesh. God has given us the capacity to make this choice. He gives us a sound mind to make the correct choices if we seek Him for one.

Who hath put wisdom in the inward parts? or who hath given <u>understanding to the heart (mind)</u>?
(Job 38:36 KJV)

For to be <u>carnally minded</u> is death; but to be <u>spiritually minded</u> is life and peace. Because <u>the carnal mind</u> is enmity against God: for it is not subject to the law of God, neither indeed can be. So then they that are in the flesh cannot please God.
(Romans 8:6-8 KJV)

But turning and seeing his disciples, he rebuked Peter and said, "Get behind me, Satan! For you are <u>not setting your mind</u> on the things of God, but on the things of man."
(Mark 8:33 ESV)

Whose end is destruction, whose God is their belly, and whose glory is in their shame, <u>who mind earthly things</u>. (Philippians 3:19 KJV)

Let no man beguile you of your reward in a voluntary humility and worshipping of angels, intruding into those things which he hath not seen, vainly puffed up by his <u>fleshly mind</u>.
(Colossians 2:18 KJV)

When individuals have made the decision in their mind to keep rebelling against God and continue in a life of sin then the result is a mind totally controlled by the carnal desires of the flesh and the world's desires and wishes. This is a very serious condition, and it is not difficult to spot. The psychology of the sinfully minded individual has shifted from God control (if they were indeed saved to begin with) to carnal control. These verses point to the drastic change in behavior that is a result of the choice to sin and turn away from God.

For the fool speaks folly, and his heart <u>(mind) is busy</u> with iniquity, to practice ungodliness, to utter error concerning the LORD.
(Isaiah 32:6a ESV)

And even as they did not like to retain God in their knowledge, God gave them over to a <u>reprobate mind</u>, to do those things which are not convenient; being filled with all unrighteousness, fornication, wickedness, covetousness, maliciousness; full of envy, murder, debate, deceit, malignity; whisperers, backbiters, haters of God, despiteful, proud, boasters, inventors of evil things, disobedient to parents, without understanding, covenantbreakers, without natural affection, implacable, unmerciful: Who knowing the judgment of God, that they which commit such things are worthy of death, not only do the same, but have pleasure in them that do them.
(Romans 1:28-32 KJV)

*I find then a law, that, when I would do good, evil is present with me. For I delight in the law of God after the inward man: <u>But I see another law in my members, warring against the law of my mind</u>, and bringing me into captivity to the law of sin which is in my members. O wretched man that I am! who shall deliver me from the body of this death?
I thank God through Jesus Christ our Lord. <u>So then with the mind I myself serve the law of God; but with the flesh the law of sin</u>.*
(Romans 7:21-25 KJV)

If any man teach otherwise, and consent not to wholesome words, even the words of our Lord Jesus Christ, and to the doctrine which is according to godliness; He is proud, knowing nothing, but doting about questions and strifes of words, whereof cometh envy, strife, railings, evil surmisings, Perverse disputings of men of <u>corrupt minds</u>, and destitute of the truth, supposing that

gain is godliness: from such withdraw thyself.
(1 Timothy 6:3-5 KJV)

Our mind is the processing function in our brains from which **all** choices come. We have the option and can choose good or evil at any moment. To willingly choose evil over and over again is to set a process in motion that will lead an individual on a path to destruction and/or hell. The power of our minds can be used for Godly good or satanic sin.

They search out injustice, saying, "We have accomplished a diligent search." For the inward mind and heart of a man are deep!
(Psalm 64:6 ESV)

For they have consulted together with one consent (mind): they are confederate against thee.
(Psalm 83:5 KJV)

And that ye study to be quiet, and to do (mind) your own business, and to work with your own hands, as we commanded you;That ye may walk honestly toward them that are without, and that ye may have lack of nothing.
(1 Thessalonians 4:11-12 KJV)

The Cure

God's Spirit and His Word can bring health to a mind and psychology that has become troubled with sin. It is a choice to return to God and obey Him. God's love for us does not stop when we rebel against Him. He is the God of restoration, for the whole man including the mind:

Jesus said unto him, Thou shalt love the Lord thy God with all thy heart, and with all thy soul, and with all thy mind. This is the first and great commandment.
(Matthew 22:37-38 KJV)

Behaviorism

Behaviorism states that humans can be trained, or conditioned, to respond in specific ways to specific stimuli and that given the correct stimuli, the personalities and behaviors of individuals, and even entire civilizations, can be controlled.

Edward Thorndike (1874-1949) initially proposed that humans and animals acquire behaviors through the association of stimuli and responses. Ivan Pavlov's (1849-1936) groundbreaking work on classical conditioning (using dogs) also provided an observable way to study behavior. The birth of modern behaviorism was championed early in the 20th century by a psychologist at Johns Hopkins University named John Watson. Watson rejected Freudian psychoanalytical developmental theories that many people found disturbing. Watson's scheme rejected all of the hidden, unconscious, and suppressed longings that Freudians attributed to behaviors and posited that humans respond to punishments and rewards. Behavior that elicits positive responses is reinforced and continued, while behavior that elicits negative responses is eliminated.

Later, the behaviorist approach was taken up by B.F. Skinner (1904-1990) who deduced the evolution of human behavior by observing the behavior of rats in a maze. Skinner wrote a novel, *Walden Two,* about a Utopian society where human behavior is governed totally by self-interested decisions based on increasing pleasure. The book led many to believe that behaviorism could indeed produce such a society.

***

Behaviorism leaves the control of the mind completely out of the picture. It is in complete opposition to the Bible. It involves the seeking of pleasure to satisfy the carnal nature of man. God asks us to control that nature, not seek to reward it.

I beseech you therefore, brethren, by the mercies of God, that ye present your bodies a living sacrifice, holy, acceptable unto God, which is your reasonable service. And be not conformed to this world: but be ye transformed by <u>the renewing of your mind</u>, that ye may prove what is that good, and acceptable, and perfect, will of God. (Romans 12:1-2 KJV)

*Husbands, love your wives, even as Christ also loved the church, and gave himself for it;
That he might sanctify and cleanse it with <u>the washing of water by the word</u>, That he might present it to himself a glorious church, not having spot, or wrinkle, or any such thing; but that it should be holy and without blemish.* (Ephesians 5:25-27 KJV)

In Ephesians 5:26 the phrase "washing with water through the word" indicates that the cleansing application of the word of God will transform the believer. We can choose to be in fellowship and be washed by God's Word daily. The result is a glimpse of the peace that Adam and Eve had before sinning. Unfortunately, individuals will often choose to let their body or worldly pleasures rule in their life. This brings about much pain and struggle.

The following list of scriptures on the mind is presented to further support the understanding of the range of function and decision making that God has given to us. As you read through the list notice how clear the understanding of the mind becomes. We are to have the mind of Christ and that requires continual time in God's Word and obedience to His Will.

Types of minds found in the Bible:

Troubled
> *And it came to pass in the morning that his spirit (mind) was troubled; and he sent and called for all the magicians of Egypt, . . .*
> (Genesis 41:8a KJV)

Understanding,
> *Yet the LORD hath not given you an heart (mind) to perceive (understand), and eyes to see, and ears to hear, unto this day.*
> (Deuteronomy 29:4 KJV)

Wise,
> *And here is the mind which hath wisdom. The seven heads are seven mountains, on which the woman sitteth.*
> (Revelations 17:9 KJV)

Willing,
> *And thou, Solomon my son, know thou the God of thy father, and serve him with a perfect heart and with a willing mind.*
> (1 Chronicles 28:9a KJV)

Out of your mind,
> *They said to her, "You are out of your mind." But she kept insisting that it was so, and they kept saying, "It is his angel!"*
> (Acts 12:15 ESV)

> *While Paul was saying this in his defense, Festus said in a loud voice, "Paul, you are out of your mind! Your great learning is driving you mad."*
> (Acts 26:24 NASB)

Right or Healthy,
> *And they come to Jesus, and see him that was possessed with the devil, and had the legion, sitting, and clothed, and in his right mind: and they were afraid.*
> (Mark 5:15 KJV)

Convinced,
> *One man esteemeth one day above another: another esteemeth every day alike. Let every man be fully persuaded in his own mind.*
> (Romans 14:5 KJV)

United in,
> *Now I beseech you, brethren, by the name of our Lord Jesus Christ, that ye all speak the same thing, and that there be no divisions among you; but that ye be perfectly joined together in the same mind and in the same judgment.* (1 Corinthians 1:10 KJV)

Made up,
> *Nevertheless he that standeth stedfast in his heart, having no necessity, but hath power over his own will, and hath so decreed in his heart (made up his mind) that he will keep his virgin, doeth well.* (1 Corinthians 7:37 KJV)

Unfruitful,
> *Wherefore let him that speaketh in an unknown tongue pray that he may interpret. For if I pray in an unknown tongue, my spirit prayeth, but my understanding (mind) is unfruitful.* (1 Corinthians 14:13-14 KJV)

Of one,
> *Finally, brethren, farewell. Be perfect, be of good comfort, be of one mind, live in peace; and the God of love and peace shall be with you.* (2 Corinthians 13:11 KJV)

The effects of alcohol abuse on the mind:

> *Do not look on the wine when it is red, When it sparkles in the cup, When it goes down smoothly; At the last it bites like a serpent And stings like a viper. Your eyes will see strange things And your mind will utter perverse things.* (Proverbs 23:31-33 NASB)

The following excerpts from Daniel tell of the involvement of the mind with the Lord. It speaks to the power of God and the choices of man.

> *In the second year of the reign of Nebuchadnezzar, Nebuchadnezzar had dreams; his spirit (mind) was troubled, and his sleep left him.* (Daniel 2:1 ESV)

> *Daniel answered in the presence of the king, and said, The secret which the king hath demanded cannot the wise men, the astrologers, the magicians, the soothsayers, shew unto the king; But there is a God in heaven that revealeth secrets, and maketh known to the king Nebuchadnezzar what shall be in the latter days. Thy dream, and the visions of thy head upon thy bed, are these; As for thee, O king, <u>thy thoughts came into thy mind</u> upon thy bed, what should come to pass hereafter: and he that revealeth secrets maketh known to thee what shall come to pass.*
> *But as for me, this secret is not revealed to me for any wisdom that I have more than any living, but for their sakes that shall make known the interpretation to the king, and that thou mightest know <u>the thoughts of thy heart (mind)</u>.* (Daniel 2:27-30 KJV)

> *I saw a dream that made me afraid. As I lay in bed the fancies and the visions of my head (mind) alarmed me. Let his mind be changed from a man's, and let a beast's mind be given to him; and let seven periods of time pass over him.* (Daniel 4:5, 16 ESV)

> *Because <u>an excellent spirit (mind)</u>, knowledge, and understanding to interpret dreams, explain riddles, and solve problems were found in this Daniel, whom the king named Belteshazzar. Now let Daniel be called, and he will show the interpretation.*

He (Nebuchadnezzar) was driven from among the children of mankind, and his mind was made like that of a beast, and his dwelling was with the wild donkeys. He was fed grass like an ox, and his body was wet with the dew of heaven, until he knew that the Most High God rules the kingdom of mankind and sets over it whom he will. (Daniel 5:12, 21 ESV)

Then said he unto me, Fear not, Daniel: for from the first day that thou didst set thine heart (mind) to understand, and to chasten thyself before thy God, thy words were heard, and I am come for thy words. (Daniel 10:12 KJV)

TOOLS FOR OVERCOMING

Giving Counsel for the Mind

Biblical counseling can be conceptualized as a process that involves helping individuals understand, control, and discipline the mind. All born again believers need to understand that being made in the image of God means that we must choose either the sinful or the Godly in life. As with the thoughts and thinking (processes in the mind), the mind's working is a gift from God that is to be used to glorify Him. God does not lie, nor does He give us impossible tasks to accomplish. We can take every thought captive in obedience to Christ Jesus. The Holy Spirit dwelling within us gives us the power and ability to do all things through Christ who strengthens us. Everyone that is counseled will have the power in his or her choices to be free from suffering. Too often people are a prisoner in their own minds. The truth does set us free from that bondage. When someone believes that they are a victim of their own thoughts and mind, the Word of God concerning the power of the mind and humble prayer, opens the door and sets the captives free.

In Sum

The animals of the world are given minds that can only do what has been programmed by the Creator to do. We, however, are made in the image of God and have a mind able to do and choose as we desire. God desires only good for us, but we do not have the capacity of good apart from Him. Left to our own desires we will choose the very things that can result in our destruction. We must seek the Mind of Christ and the freedom that comes from giving Him the control of our life and will.

Chapter 6:

THE HEART: OUR MORAL NATURE

*The heart is deceitful above all things, and desperately wicked: who can know it?
I the LORD search the heart, I try the reins, even to give every man according to his ways, and according to the fruit of his doings.*
(Jeremiah 17:9-10 KJV)

Whenever we are asked the question, "Who are you?" we typically give our name. But our name is simply a family identification label and does not give much information about who or what we are. In the past two chapters we studied the foundation of mental activity or thoughts, as well as the controlling function of the mind. Now we will examine what God tells us is the core of who we are - the Heart.

The clearest way that we can be identified is by the expressions (verbal and behavioral) that come out of our heart. The heart is the core expression of our complex moral nature (Christ's nature if you are seeking it), our emotions and motivations. The fallen moral nature of man is forever changed when we ask Jesus into our hearts to transform us, to save us from our sins and to become part of His family. The regenerative power of the Holy Spirit is expressed in His ability to transform us to be able to stand in the presence of a Holy God. This is a change of heart.

Changing the heart is the key to the lasting change that reflects our spiritual and moral development. As individuals who disciple and counsel, we are involved with God's process of illuminating and changing hearts. We have no capacity to make the change, but do help individuals in the Body of Christ learn how to pray for and seek God for the changes that are needed.

Our hearts are the seats of our emotions, personality, morality, and in combination with the mind, our understanding. In the days of the old Hebrew writers they used the term heart for all of these core aspects of our psychology. This may have been because of the physiological experiences that we have in our physical heart when a psychologically powerful event occurs. Hormones and other neural chemical events take place when strong emotions or experiences happen. These chemical messengers trigger changes in heart rate and vascular activity. All emotions occur after thoughts that come into the mind. This interconnectedness of thoughts, mind and heart form the basis of our psychology, including all emotional experiences.

> *Changing the heart is the key to the lasting change that reflects our spiritual and moral development*

As with all of the elements of man, the heart is part of being made in the image of God. We have the same heart element but it lacks God's moral nature. The Bible tells us about God's heart:

God's heart can feel pain:

And it repented the LORD that he had made man on the earth, <u>and it grieved him at his heart.</u>
(Genesis 6:6 KJV)

God has thoughts, word and speech in His heart:

And the LORD smelled a sweet savour; and <u>the LORD said in his heart,</u> I will not again curse the ground any more for man's sake; for the imagination of man's heart is evil from his youth; neither will I again smite any more every thing living, as I have done.
(Genesis 8:21 KJV)

We are the focus of His Heart:

> *And the LORD said unto him, I have heard thy prayer and thy supplication, that thou hast made before me: I have hallowed this house, which thou hast built, to put my name there for ever; and mine eyes and <u>mine heart shall be there perpetually</u>.*
> (1 Kings 9:3 KJV)

The heart is the point in our human construction that we can draw closest to God. It is the condition of our hearts that matters most, and God is the only one who truly knows and understands what is in the heart of man.

> *But the LORD said unto Samuel, Look not on his countenance, or on the height of his stature; because I have refused him: for the LORD seeth not as man seeth; for man looketh on the outward appearance, but <u>the LORD looketh on the heart</u>.*
> (1 Samuel 16:7 KJV)

Only God knows what is in our hearts:

> *Then hear thou in heaven thy dwelling place, and forgive, and do, and give to every man according to his ways, <u>whose heart thou knowest; (for thou, even thou only, knowest the hearts of all the children of men;)</u> That they may fear thee all the days that they live in the land which thou gavest unto our fathers.*
> (1 Kings 8:39-40 KJV)

> *Then hear thou from heaven thy dwelling place, and forgive, and render unto every man according unto all his ways, <u>whose heart thou knowest; (for thou only knowest the hearts of the children of men:)</u>*
> (2 Chronicles 6:30 KJV)

God has the power to change our hearts.

> *And it was so, that when he had turned his back to go from Samuel, <u>God gave him another heart</u>: and all those signs came to pass that day.*
> (1 Samuel 10:9 KJV)

God wants us to seek and to know His Heart.

> *But now thy kingdom shall not continue: the LORD hath sought him a man after his own heart, and the LORD hath commanded him to be captain over his people, because thou hast not kept that which the LORD commanded thee.*
> (1 Samuel 13:14 KJV)

> *And I will give you pastors according to mine heart, which shall feed you with knowledge and understanding.*
> (Jeremiah 3:15 KJV)

These scriptures point out that God wants us to make it the focus of our lives to understand Him. A good leader is distinguished from others by his or her desire to know and understand what God desires. Keeping His commandments and following Christ is what is required of us in order to be used by God. He will test the true condition of our hearts by testing to see if our word and behavior match up.

> *And thou shalt remember all the way which the LORD thy God led thee these forty years in the wilderness, to humble thee, and to prove thee, to know what was in thine heart, whether thou wouldest keep his commandments, or no.*
> (Deuteronomy 8:2 KJV)

We have to keep in mind that we may say one thing and do something else. Paul spoke of this as a source of frustration (Rom. 7:14-20). In times of testing, God will stand back and see if we follow through. We may also see this testing in the life of a believer when we evaluate to see if their words fit their behavior. It was clear that the Pharisees and teachers of the law did not practice what they preached in Jesus' time. The behavior often shows the heart while the words give the "right" impression.

The mind and the heart are not the same

Both the mind and heart have thoughts. It is important to remember that the mind has a decision making function. It makes decisions about our thoughts and behaviors. Based upon information from many sources our mind will decide. We can decide in our mind if any thought is "Right by Christ." This includes thoughts from the heart.

> *And thou, Solomon my son, know thou the God of thy father, and serve him with a perfect heart and with a willing mind: for the LORD searcheth all hearts, and understandeth all the imaginations of the thoughts: if thou seek him, he will be found of thee; but if thou forsake him, he will cast thee off for ever.*
> (1 Chronicles 28:9 KJV)

> *I know also, my God, that thou triest the heart, and hast pleasure in uprightness. As for me, in the uprightness of mine heart I have willingly offered all these things: and now have I seen with joy thy people, which are present here, to offer willingly unto thee.*
> (1 Chronicles 29:17 KJV)

The foundation of our will is in our heart, but decisions regarding our will come from the mind. Our true intent comes from our heart but decisions to act upon our intent come from our mind. Remember the command from the previous chapter to "take every thought captive?" Every thought includes the ones from our heart.

Emotions can occur in our heart (the core of our being) and they have a very powerful impact on our behavior and lives.

> *And the anger of the LORD was kindled against Moses, and he said, Is not Aaron the Levite thy brother? I know that he can speak well. And also, behold, he cometh forth to meet thee: and when he seeth thee, he will be <u>glad in his heart</u>.*
> (Exodus 4:14 KJV)

> *You shall <u>not hate your brother in your heart</u>, but you shall reason frankly with your neighbor, lest you incur sin because of him.*
> (Leviticus 19:17 ESV)

> *And when Saul saw the host of the Philistines, he was afraid, and <u>his heart greatly trembled</u>.*
> (1 Samuel 28:5 KJV)

> *On the eighth day he sent the people away: and they blessed the king, and went unto their tents joyful and <u>glad of heart</u> for all the goodness that the LORD had done for David his servant, and for Israel his people.*
> (1 Kings 8:66 KJV)

> *And on the three and twentieth day of the seventh month he sent the people away into their tents, <u>glad and merry in heart</u> for the goodness that the LORD had shewed unto David, and to Solomon, and to Israel his people.* (2 Chronicles 7:10 KJV)

The physiological experience of strong heartfelt emotions can cause us to leap for joy or to faint or have weak and shaking legs. When we experience a very fearful event we can receive such a strong surge of neural chemicals that we collapse, run, or just shake from the dosage. Panic and anxiety disorders typically come about from repeated inaccurate thoughts in the mind that cause strong emotions in the heart. As adults we do have a choice of what to put into our hearts:

> *Pharaoh turned and went into his house, and he <u>did not take even this to heart</u>.*
> (Exodus 7:23 ESV)

And David <u>took these words to heart</u> and was much afraid of Achish the king of Gath.
(1 Samuel 21:12 KJV)

Then Absalom her brother said to her, "Has Amnon your brother been with you? But now keep silent, my sister, he is your brother; <u>do not take this matter to heart</u>."
(2 Samuel 13:20a NASB)

In the case of King David above (Isa. 21:12), words were taken seriously (to heart) and the result was great fear. Other times taking something to heart means that we believe that we have been changed by an action or statement of others. After Tamar was raped by her half-brother Amnon, her brother Absalom encouraged her to not let his sin stain who she was, or don't take it to heart.

Our heart will cause us to take actions that are good and just:

Speak unto the children of Israel, that they bring me an offering: of every man that <u>giveth it willingly with his heart</u> ye shall take my offering.
(Exodus 25:2 KJV)

And they came, every one whose <u>heart stirred him up</u>, and every one whom his spirit made willing, and they brought the LORD's offering to the work of the tabernacle of the congregation, and for all his service, and for the holy garments.
(Exodus 35:21 KJV)

<u>We are motivated by desires in our hearts</u>. The desire to go on in life with tasks great and small comes from our hearts. Most of our behaviors arise from the motivations that we have in our hearts.

Whither shall we go up? our brethren have <u>discouraged our heart</u>, saying, The people is greater and taller than we; the cities are great and walled up to heaven; and moreover we have seen the sons of the Anakims there.
(Deuteronomy 1:28 KJV)

And David said to Saul, <u>Let no man's heart fail</u> because of him; thy servant will go and fight with this Philistine.
(1 Samuel 17:32 KJV)

And Abner said unto David, I will arise and go, and will gather all Israel unto my lord the king, that they may make a league with thee, and that thou mayest reign over <u>all that thine heart desireth</u>. And David sent Abner away; and he went in peace.
(2 Samuel 3:21 KJV)

So I will take you, and you shall reign over <u>all your heart desires</u>, and you shall be king over Israel.
(1 Kings 11:37 NKJV)

The heart of man is truly the core of our existence. Many of the most important descriptors of the heart are found in Proverbs and Psalms. See Appendix C for scriptures about the heart from Proverbs, and Appendix D for the scriptures from Psalms (you are encouraged to read all of these scriptures to gain a clear understanding of the heart).

TOOLS FOR OVERCOMING

Counseling the Heart

There are 541 occurrences of the term heart and 201 occurrences of hearts in the Bible (NIV; all other versions are very similar on these terms). These 742 scriptures point to the importance of the heart in managing our lives and identifying who we are. This collection of teaching from God also points to the poor condition of our hearts when we are not in Christ Jesus. Knowledge and wisdom from the Word will cause our Christian hearts to be strengthened, and our old personalities to pass away as we are made new. The changed heart, through accepting Jesus as Lord and Savior is the foundation of who we are. Yet, Christians have problems that stem from their heart. We become overwhelmed by circumstances and take things to heart that cause us to lose heart. Sometimes individuals give up on life and God. By learning the scriptures on the heart we are prepared to listen to others and see, based on the wisdom of God's Word, what the core (heart) issue is. God will sometimes tell us what is in the heart of another.

> *And Samuel answered Saul, and said, I am the seer: go up before me unto the high place; for ye shall eat with me to day, and to morrow I will let thee go, and will tell thee <u>all that is in thine heart</u>.* (1 Samuel 9:19 KJV)

This knowing or being a "seer" is something that occurs at the will of God, not man. Demonic spiritual forces can provide information about another individual for the purpose of glorifying satan. This is the work of a medium or witch. No Christian is to ever participate in this activity. Most of the individuals to whom we give counsel will be stuck in their situations. They often fail to understand the motivations of their heart and how it causes the repeated behavior.

Sometimes we can become stuck in our circumstances when our heart fails us because of fear:

> *But it came to pass in the morning, when the wine was gone out of Nabal, and his wife had told him these things, that <u>his heart died within him</u>, and he became as a stone.* (1 Samuel 25:37 KJV)

Often our attitudes toward others are based on a response our heart has for that person.

> *Michal Saul's daughter looked through a window, and saw king David leaping and dancing before the LORD; and <u>she despised him in her heart</u>.* (2 Samuel 6:16b KJV)

> *Now Joab the son of Zeruiah perceived that <u>the king's heart was toward Absalom</u>.* (2 Samuel 14:1 KJV)

Depression and anxiety come from a condition that develops in our hearts. This condition may be from some outside act or influence, but it is in the heart or our core that the deep emotional disturbance takes place. All of the anger, bitterness and hatred towards others that stems from unforgiveness also come from a condition that is in the heart. But, just as the heart is the place where negative issues are seated, it is the place of integrity and strength:

> *And Solomon said, Thou hast shewed unto thy servant David my father great mercy, according as he walked before thee in truth, and in righteousness, and in <u>uprightness of heart</u> with thee.* (1 Kings 3:6a KJV)

> *And if thou wilt walk before me, as David thy father walked, <u>in integrity of heart, and in uprightness</u>, to do according to all that I have commanded thee, and wilt keep my statutes and my judgments.* (1 Kings 9:4 KJV)

> *My words shall be of <u>the uprightness of my heart</u>: and my lips shall utter knowledge clearly.* (Job 33:3 KJV)

Curing the condition of the heart is the job for the healing power of the Word of God and His Holy Spirit. In providing counsel and discipleship our understanding of the truth regarding God's power is vital. We can pray or lead others in a prayer to ask God for changes in the heart:

> *Give therefore thy servant an understanding heart to judge thy people, that I may discern between good and bad: for who is able to judge this thy so great a people?* (1 Kings 3:9 KJV)

> *Behold, I have done according to thy words: lo, I have given thee <u>a wise and an understanding heart</u>; so that there was none like thee before thee, neither after thee shall any arise like unto thee.* (1 Kings 3:12 KJV)

> *And all the earth sought to Solomon, to hear <u>his wisdom, which God had put in his heart</u>.* (1 Kings 10:24 KJV)

The Word states that when two or more of us are gathered in His name, He us there with us. When a Christian counselor and Christian client are together God is present. In the presence of God we will know what is troubling our heart:

> *What prayer and supplication soever be made by any man, or by all thy people Israel, which <u>shall know every man the plague of his own heart</u>, and spread forth his hands toward this house: Then hear thou in heaven thy dwelling place,* (1 Kings 8:38-39a)

When giving counsel to an individual with a particular sin issue the process of confession, repentance and turning back toward God are the steps that need to occur in order for restoration to occur and the heart to be healed from the sin.

> *Yet if they bethink themselves in the land whither they are carried captive, and turn and pray unto thee in the land of their captivity, saying, We have sinned, we have done amiss, and have dealt wickedly; <u>if they return to thee with all their heart</u> and with all their soul in the land of their captivity, whither they have carried them captives, and pray toward their land, which thou gavest unto their fathers, and toward the city which thou hast chosen, and toward the house which I have built for thy name:* (2 Chronicles 6:37-38 KJV)

When we fail to keep our hearts on God we will typically end up involved in evil behavior:

> *And he did evil, because <u>he prepared not his heart</u> to seek the LORD.* (2 Chronicles 12:14 KJV)

Changes in the heart involve a decision on the part of the Christian to seek God:

> *And they entered into a covenant to seek the LORD God of their fathers with all their heart and with all their soul (mind).* (2 Chronicles 15:12 KJV)

Often scriptures are overlooked that indicate how pleased our heavenly Father is when we make the decision to focus on seeking Him with our heart, even in the face of ongoing error. These scriptures further confirm how important the choice is to seek God in the process of counseling:

> *Nevertheless there are good things found in thee, in that thou hast taken away the groves out of the land, and hast <u>prepared thine heart</u> to seek God.*
> (2 Chronicles 19:3 KJV)

> *And he sought Ahaziah: and they caught him, (for he was hid in Samaria,) and brought him to Jehu: and when they had slain him, they buried him: Because, said they, he is the son of Jehoshaphat, who <u>sought the LORD with all his heart</u>. So the house of Ahaziah had no power to keep still the kingdom.*
> (2 Chronicles 22:9 KJV)

> *That <u>prepareth his heart to seek God</u>, the LORD God of his fathers, though he be not cleansed according to the purification of the sanctuary. And the LORD hearkened to Hezekiah, and healed the people.*
> (2 Chronicles 30:19-20 KJV)

Yes, even if we are making mistakes, God still will bless us if we are truly seeking Him. This is not an excuse to keep making the mistakes. It is simply an indication of the difference between our mind and heart. If our heart is right, seeking God, and with our mind we make a poor choice, then it represents the truth of our fallen nature.

When working with individuals with ongoing sin it must be made clear to them that the heart must change. They must respond to God's Word and the conscience's nudges of the Holy Spirit:

> *But Hezekiah rendered not again according to the benefit done unto him; for <u>his heart was lifted up</u>: therefore there was wrath upon him, and upon Judah and Jerusalem. Notwithstanding Hezekiah humbled himself <u>for the pride of his heart</u>, both he and the inhabitants of Jerusalem, so that the wrath of the LORD came not upon them in the days of Hezekiah.* (2 Chronicles 32:25-26 KJV)

This also requires action on their part:

> *Because <u>thine heart was tender</u>, and thou didst <u>humble thyself</u> before God, when thou heardest his words against this place, and against the inhabitants thereof, and humbledst thyself before me, and didst rend thy clothes, and weep before me; I have even heard thee also, saith the LORD.* (2 Chronicles 34:27 KJV)

Obeying God is an act of submission and humility. Those hard in heart, who have turned from God, will not change unless they respond to the Counselor's (Holy Spirit) plea.

> *And he also rebelled against king Nebuchadnezzar, who had made him swear by God: but he stiffened his neck, and <u>hardened his heart</u> from turning unto the LORD God of Israel.* (2 Chronicles 36:13 KJV)

As counselors and ministers of truth we can only say the Word of God. The mind of the individuals that we are discipling must choose to take the Word to heart and obey it.

Humanistic Psychology

Humanistic psychology occurred as a reaction to Freudian (psychoanalysis) and behaviorism (Darwinism), both of which over-psychologize and dehumanize man. Around 1960, an assembly of American psychologists began to feel that these two theories lacked the insight that *man is also spirit*. Humanistic psychology emphasizes *understanding* the individual, more than seeking to "explain" it or to predict its reactions. It holds the view that man is complex and cannot be reduced to psychological mechanisms (psychoanalysis), bio-chemical processes or outer sociological determinations (behaviorism).

Humanistic psychology stresses that man is different from animals because he has *reason* and *free will*. The world forms the individual, and the individual can influence his or her environment - and man forms his or her own life, since *life values* and *personal goals* differ from person to person (**relativism**). One of the tasks of humanistic psychology is to bring the individual in contact with his or her own original and *authentic nature. So*, it follows that man's alienation from nature, fellow human beings, and society, not to mention himself or herself is one of the main challenges, of psychotherapy.

Humanistic psychology was developed in the grounds of European humanism and European existence philosophy. Many of the founders belonged to Protestant Christendom, for example, Søren Kierkegaard, Ludwig Binswanger, Martin Heidegger, Paul Johannes Tillich, and Karl Jaspers - but also others with a background in Judaism, Catholicism, communism or atheism such as Albert Camus, Edmund Husserl, Martin Buber, Friedrich Nietzsche, Gabriel Marcel, Jean-Paul Sartre, and others. The pioneer of Humanistic Psychology, Abraham Maslow was (like Rollo May) inspired by Zen Buddhism and Taoism. Maslow concluded, that every person has a potential of ***self-realization (become God)***, once the basic, physiological needs have been covered. Terms like meaning, self-actualization, authenticity, life values, and motivation for growth are therefore characteristic of humanistic psychology vocabulary.

Note: It sounds good on the surface, but humanistic psychology is the most dangerous and demonic of all counseling forms. Whatever you really want in life should be yours (man has the power). It looks like an angel of light, but it represents the deep darkness of man's self-centered thought. It is man-centered psychology in opposition to the truth that we have a God-centered psychology.

In Sum

Our heart is the core of our expressive self. It must be transformed by the Spirit of God in order for us to have a life of integrity and consistency in our walk with God. It is the way of man to seek joy and peace in life. Yet, the true happiness does not arrive from exercising the evil that is the motivation in one's heart. It only comes from seeking the source of all good things with all of our hearts. When we give counsel and disciple others there is no stronger encouragement than to let go of our desires and seek His. We are the desire of His heart and He should be the desire of ours.

Chapter 7:

MADE IN THE IMAGE OF GOD: FULLY CONSCIOUS, FULLY AWARE

*There is therefore now no condemnation to them
which are in Christ Jesus...* (Romans 8:1a KJV)
*Therefore, if anyone is in Christ he is a new creation;
old things have passed away; behold,
all things have become new.* (2 Corinthians 5:17 NKJV)

The world with its evolutionary belief equates us along with the animals, whereas God in Genesis 1:26-28 places us in authority over all the animals. We are created in the image of God and not related to the animals. No more clearly is this fact articulated as in the truth that we are fully conscious, or fully aware. No animal has ever sinned nor have they felt guilt. Therefore, they have no need of a Savior.

It is our fully aware consciousness that places us under conviction when we have sinned and rises to self-condemnation when we fail to repent. The sin of a godly man or woman instantly leads to an awareness of the separation from God and subsequent pain of that separation and conviction of the Holy Spirit's action within our heart (core of our being).

It would make no sense for a Creator to hold us accountable for that which we cannot be aware of. Our conscious awareness is perhaps the greatest gift contained within the blessing of being made in the image of God.

Animal awareness is limited to biological function. Their joy is in their stomachs, procreation, and physical comfort. On the other hand, we can experience unspeakable joy in the midst of intolerable storm and discomfort. We are told to crucify, or put to death, our flesh.

*And they that are Christ's have
crucified the flesh with the affections
and lusts.*
(Galatians 5:24 KJV)

If man were an animal, we would therefore cease to exist as our flesh ceases. But in God's image, it is only upon the death of the flesh that we may truly live. This ability to subjugate and control the cravings of the flesh is the expression of our conscious awareness and our sonship to the Father in Heaven.

> This act of conscious awareness enables the crucifixion of the flesh and the identification and resistance to the works of Satan.

*For if ye live after the
flesh, ye shall die: but if
ye through the Spirit do
mortify the deeds of the
body, ye shall live. For as
many as are led by the
Spirit of God, they are
the sons of God.*
(Romans 8:13-14 KJV)

We learned from the chapter on thoughts the need (command) to take every thought captive to the obedience of Christ. This act of conscious awareness enables the crucifixion of the flesh and the identification and resistance to the works of Satan. Alone, this is impossible, but with Christ Jesus this is accomplished and our freedom from the bondage of the flesh and Satan are assured (Gal 6:14). With our mind we are able to choose and identify that which is of God and that which is of the evil one. The Apostle Paul presents the fallen dilemma most elegantly when he says:

*For the good that I would I do not:
but the evil which I would not, that I
do.* (Romans 7:19 KJV)

This is the expression of our fallen nature, our flaws from The Fall. Even though we are fully conscious, apart from Christ Jesus, our Lord and Savior, there is no hope, and we will become like the animals. But as Paul exclaims:

> *O wretched man that I am! who shall deliver me from the body of this death? I thank God through Jesus Christ our Lord. So then with the mind I myself serve the law of God; but with the flesh the law of sin.*
> (Romans 7:24-25 KJV)

We are indeed made in the image of God, but the fall of man necessitated the blood of the Lamb for the restoration of man. In the next chapter the profound impact of the family of origin upon the psychology of man will be presented. The teaching in those early years can help us to understand how we are constructed, or increase the shackles that hold us in sin by denying our consciousness. Not being aware of our responsibility for our thoughts perpetuates responses like "the devil made me do it" as a reaction to our own sin.

Free Will?

The free will of man is often misunderstood. It is a co-existent gift with being fully conscious and aware. With the gift of free will, love is powerful and pure. Without it, it is a genetically programmed response (the kitty or puppy's behavior). The two great commands that sum up all of the Law and Prophets epitomize the power of free will and the choice to love (Matt 22:37-40). Embedded within the command to love God is the recognition that God our Father is our Creator, and above us in all things (the Authority in life). The command to love our neighbor as our self demonstrates the choice to value others. The "new commandment" displays the choice to value others more than ourselves (John 13:34-35).

With our free will we choose to accept Christ as Lord and Savior, thus giving up our free will for His. To reject Christ is to give up our free will for satan and evil. Free will is set aside for God's will in order to find peace and happiness that is eternal.

Our free will is the basis for the cry that is so often heard when suffering strikes our lives; "Why did God allow this to happen to me?" Free will requires responsibility. The sin and tragedy in the world is not from God; it is a result of the fall of man and sinful behavior exercised in the free will of evil man. As fallen creatures it is not possible to exercise appropriate free will apart from God.

> *Because the carnal mind is enmity against God: for it is not subject to the law of God, neither indeed can be. So then they that are in the flesh cannot please God.*
> (Romans 8:7-8 KJV)

We are to do all things as unto God. We are to choose to exercise our free will under the constraints and confines of God's law and the guiding of the Holy Spirit. We can choose what color sneakers to buy (free will), but we are to use our feet and lives to spread the Gospel of Christ Jesus (God's will).

Being fully conscious and aware is expressed in the actions of our free will choices. We choose our thoughts and behaviors. If we do not know this truth we will act irresponsibly in our lives. Often this irresponsible action is blamed upon satan or someone else. The Bible tells us that when we acknowledge God in all of our activities, He will direct our path (Pv. 3:6). We must be conscious and aware of our activities (mental and physical) in order to give them to God or acknowledge Him in the process. Many Christians live lives with no direction because of no responsibility in their thoughts, choices and actions. Their free will is flawed!

Good and Evil:

The proper exercise of our fully aware and conscious state in the function of our free will is not present at birth. It takes almost two decades of life before our physical neural mechanisms are working correctly enough to be fully aware of good and evil

> *Your carcasses shall fall in this wilderness; and all that were numbered of you, according to your whole number, from <u>twenty years old and upward</u> which have murmured against me.*
> (Numbers 14:29 KJV)

> *Moreover your little ones, which ye said should be a prey, and your*

children, <u>which in that day had no knowledge between good and evil</u>, they shall go in thither, and unto them will I give it, and they shall possess it. (Deuteronomy 1:39 KJV)

God has fixed the age of true knowledge of good from evil at 20 years and above.

> <u>Note</u>: This is not to be confused with right and wrong. The terms good and evil indicate that which is presented by another. Right and wrong is self generated. The problems seen with teenagers following the "wrong crowd" are the result of not being able to identify evil. The parents are to protect them from such individuals.

Prior to this age the physical formation of the mind is not complete and changes in hormone activity in the body prevent clear thought. This places a great responsibility upon parents to guide their children into the awareness of their thoughts and consciousness. This requires a learned awareness of God (next chapter).

In Sum:

This great gift of being made in God's image with full consciousness and awareness is a blessing that allows us to choose our directions in life. The animals only do what God has programmed them through their genetics to do. All statements that somehow accept evolution, serve to make a monkey out of God, and defile His greatest creation, man. When we fail to take responsibility for our actions, we make a monkey out of ourselves. Our fully conscious state submitted to the will of God makes for a wonderful life in Him.

I beseech you therefore, brethren, by the mercies of God, that ye present your bodies a living sacrifice, holy, acceptable unto God, which is your reasonable service. And be not conformed to this world: but be ye transformed by the renewing of your mind, that ye may prove what is that good, and acceptable, and perfect, will of God.
(Romans 12:1-2 KJV)

Chapter 8:
NURTURE: THE IMPACT OF FAMILY ON OUR PSYCHOLOGY

*Train up a child in the way he should go:
and when he is old, he will not depart from it.*
(Proverbs 22:6 KJV)

We are all born into a family. The appearance or structure of that family may be vastly different across our many individual experiences. Some have grown up in orphanages or group homes, while others have a biological father and mother who were there for them until they grew up and left home. God's plan as articulated in the Bible is that our biological families would care for us. This includes not only mother and father, but also grandparents and aunts, uncles and others.

Caring for our physical needs while developing is a very important element of our health and psychology. Providing a safe environment free from worldly fears, as well as proper nutrition and physical maintenance, allow for the tissues of the mind to form and connect into a properly functioning mental organ. These are some of the most basic responsibilities of all individuals in the parenting role in the lives of children. This set of responsibilities represents the physical element of the commands to care for our children and train them up.

Presented in the previous chapter was the Biblical guideline that we do not develop a clear sense of good and evil until we reach 20 years of age (Num 14:29; Duet 1:39). This indicates that for the first 19 years of life the parents are held responsible for the actions of the children. If God does not hold them accountable until 20, then they are not accountable. What happens between birth and age 20 is the process of training. The only Godly way of accomplishing this is in the training and admonition of God (Eph 6:4).

The family's impact on the psychology of the child can range from one that is healthy and facultative to destructive and disorganizing. The Bible tells us that parents are to bring up their children with love and proper discipline. That means teaching them right from wrong (this is different from a child being able to identify the good and evil behaviors and intentions of others).

He that spareth his rod hateth his son: but he that loveth him chasteneth him betimes.
(Proverbs 13:24 KJV)

Fathers are to be patient and gentle in their attitudes toward their children.

Fathers, provoke not your children to anger, lest they be discouraged.
(Colossians 3:21 KJV)

Parents are not to avoid the responsibility of correcting their children because it is uncomfortable. The mental stability of the child depends upon the structured instruction and discipline. In Proverbs 13:24 above the command to parents is to discipline the child promptly. There is to be a quick connection between the sin and the punishment.

The Bible tells us that we are to be proactive as parents. Many fathers and mothers miss this important point, and they will focus solely on the "rod" discipline forgetting the other important forms of instructions that are indicated.

> The Bible tells us that we are to be proactive as parents.

> *Train up a child in the way he should go.* (Proverbs 22:6a KJV)

This implies that we are to tell the child in advance as much as we are able the correct path to take in life. This will eliminate much of the need for the rod of correction. All children will test their parents with their rebellious sin nature. But, if they have not been told the correct way to go in advance, then their negative behavior may only represent their own trial and error efforts to figure things out on their own.

Mental Discipline

The processes of taking every thought captive, and understanding who they are in Christ Jesus must be modeled and taught to all children. If the parents do not understand their psychological selves, then their children will have a much harder time getting a grip on their own mental processes. If chaos is the norm in the family of origin then chaos will be the norm in the thinking of the child.

Structure and stability are paramount to the healthy mental development of children. Consistency in discipline results in a deep understanding of the connection between sin and consequences. Remember that the deception of Eve was that the serpent told her there would be no punishment. If a direct connection between sin and punishment is not made early in life, then criminal behavior may result in adulthood. Erratic physical punishment teaches that punishment is just a fact of life in the home; it is only randomly connected to their behavior and may occur at any time without reason or warning. Also, if being good (avoiding sin) does not stop the "rod" then why bother? This can be the root of a lifetime of bitterness.

> *And, ye fathers, provoke not your children to wrath: but bring them up in the nurture and admonition of the Lord.*
> (Ephesians 6:4 KJV)

The result of inconsistent physical punishment is that the individual is prone to develop a powerful sense of false guilt that may result in their mental life freezing or arresting at the childhood level. They will be filled with a sense of deep personal shame about themselves that will place them into the slavery of working for salvation and relationships. The bonds of the slavery to shame can only be broken by the truth and the Love of God.

> *Then said Jesus to those Jews which believed on him, If ye continue in my word, then are ye my disciples indeed; And ye shall know the truth, and the truth shall make you free*
> (John 8:31-32 KJV)

The goal of parents should be making sure that the children know the Savior Jesus Christ. The Bible used to be the only textbook that was used for Reading and Writing exercises in school.

> *And these words which I command you today shall be in your heart. You shall teach them diligently to your children, and shall talk of them when you sit in your house, when you walk by the way, when you lie down, and when you rise up. You shall bind them as a sign on your hand, and they shall be as frontlets between your eyes. You shall write them on the doorposts of your house and on your gates.*
> (Deuteronomy 6:6-9 NKJV)

Now the Word of God is banned as a curriculum book in public schools and seldom read in the home. The process of developing an accurate self-image requires that the child know the Creator and His love for them. The study of God's Word renews the mind and equips the individual for all good work.

> *All Scripture is given by inspiration of God, and is profitable for doctrine, for reproof, for correction, for instruction in righteousness, that the man of God may be complete, thoroughly equipped for every good work*
> (2 Timothy 3:16-17 NKJV)

If chaos is the norm in the family of origin then chaos will be the norm in the thinking of the child.

In Sum:

The psychology of the child will have a strong likelihood of being healthy and in Christ Jesus if the parents do what God requires them to do. Yet, even with atheist parents a child can know Jesus Christ and arrive in adulthood with a healthy psychology.

It is God alone in us and through us that causes the miracle of salvation to happen. The psychology of a child will equally have a strong chance of being underdeveloped and warped if that is the model they saw in their home of origin.

TOOLS FOR OVERCOMING

Counsel/Discipleship Application

Many of the individuals that we disciple or counsel will have blockages in developing a healthy psychology because of past experiences. How or why these challenges developed is helpful in constructing an understanding of the origin of dysfunctional decisions. But, knowing the truth of God's Word does not depend upon any other understanding.

> *By taking every thought captive to the obedience of Christ Jesus and renewing the mind by washing it with the Word of God, every believing individual can develop a healthy psychology.*

Many counselors make the point that the individual must somehow know what happened way back when. This is not a Biblical perspective on giving counsel or discipleship. The power of God's Word and His Holy Spirit lack nothing and need no help from anyone. Frequently the origin of the false beliefs that individuals bring in for counsel is well known. The truth of God's Word will set them free with or without any past knowledge. The knowledge can help explain, but can never change. The knowledge has value, yet lacks the power necessary to direct to the truth.

By taking every thought captive to the obedience of Christ Jesus and renewing the mind by washing it with the Word of God, every believing individual can develop a healthy psychology. They can know who they are in Jesus and live out their lives in the freedom of His Truth.

PART III:
GODLY UNDERSTANDING OF OUR EARTHY EXPERIENCE

In the previous sections of this text the construction and condition of man as presented in the Bible was discussed. We know that God has presented us a psychology of the mind that covers great detail in understanding and resolving the issues affecting our human condition. In this last section we will cover some of the psychological and emotional states that are common in our lives. Armed with the knowledge gained thus far we will look at how God wants us to think about our inner lives. Our anger, anxiety, peace and other experiences will be reviewed based on the scriptures.

As a Biblical counselor or one who disciples we need to have a clear understanding of what is normal or common to man. Many of the questions and situations that we will be presented with in counseling will simply be the result of a lack of Biblical understanding and knowledge. For example, it is common to hear someone speak of his or her anger as wrong or evil. Being angry about sin or an injustice to someone who is weak or less fortunate is a Godly anger. All Christians need to know that anger is not in and of itself a sin. It is what, who and why we are angry that make the thoughts and feelings sinful or not.

> *As a Biblical counselor or one who disciples we need to have a clear understanding of what is normal or common to man.*

By studying some of the common conditions of man found in the Bible we become more ready to help the hurting and encourage those in struggles. We will begin with anger, one of the most common and unfortunately destructive of human thoughts. It is a thought that has a very strong emotional component, but we must remember as we discuss terms in this chapter, that emotions do not exist apart from some form of thought.

As we cover the material ask yourself how would you use this information in helping people to whom you minister? Keep in mind that Jesus came to take away our sins - not our emotions.

Biblical Psychology

The Psycho-Emotional State of Anger

Is anger bad? Our first impression would be to say yes. Keep in mind that we are made in the image of God. God has anger; therefore we have the emotional and mental experiences of anger. In most cases anger is not a thought and emotion that we will want to cultivate. There are some instances when anger can be used for positive purposes, as long as it does not lead to sin. For example, anger should never be allowed to grow to the point of a physical fight or some other type of ungodly confrontation.

The definition for the word anger in Webster's dictionary reads: hostile feelings because of opposition, a hurt, etc. If something or someone opposes or goes against what we think is normal or right and causes us to experience hurt, it may manifest itself as anger.

Anger can lead us to commit many sins.

An angry man stirreth up strife, and a furious man aboundeth in transgression. (Proverbs 29:22 KJV)

Cease from anger, and forsake wrath: fret not thyself in any wise to do evil.
(Psalms 37:8 KJV)

Ye have heard that it was said of them of old time, Thou shalt not kill; and whosoever shall kill shall be in danger of the judgment: But I say unto you, That whosoever is angry with his brother without a cause shall be in danger of the council.
(Matthew 5:21-22a KJV)

Here Jesus not only equates anger with murder, He also enforces the point that anger can ultimately lead to murder. That is why Jesus says that they are equally wrong. If anger is allowed to simmer, eventually it will boil over and an even worse sin will be committed. We will become angry from time to time, but we are not to let the emotional state out of control and lead us into evil acts.

Allowing our anger to be freely expressed without first taking the thoughts captive and governing our speech or behavior can lead us away from God.

Wherefore, my beloved brethren, let every man be swift to hear, slow to speak, slow wrath: For the wrath of man worketh not the righteousness of God.
(James 1:19-20 KJV)

The more we wallow in and concentrate our anger, the farther we move from the righteous path that God wants us to stay on. Our psychology becomes consumed with thoughts of anger and justice. In contrast, God tells us to rid ourselves of anger. We are to forgive those who sin against us and make us angry, or let go of our right to justice and compensation.

> The more we wallow in and concentrate our anger, the farther we move from the righteous path that God wants us to stay on.

Let all bitterness, and wrath, and anger, and clamour, and evil speaking, be put away from you, with all malice: And be ye kind one to one another, tenderhearted, forgiving one another, even as God for Christ's sake hath forgiven you. (Eph 4:31-32 KJV)

Ye have heard that it hath been said, Thou shalt love thy neighbor, and hate thine enemy. But I say unto you, Love your enemies, bless them that curse you, do good to them that hate you, and pray for them which despitefully use you, and persecute you; That ye may sons of your Father which is in heaven: for he maketh his sun to rise on the evil and on the good, and sendeth rain on the just and on the unjust. For if ye love them which love you, what reward

> *have ye? Do not even the publicans the same?*
> (Matthew 5:43-46 KJV)

Jesus tells us to forgive all those who do us wrong whether they are enemies or friends. We have been forgiven by God, so we must do the same to others. If we cannot fully forgive others then we must not fully understand the forgiveness that God has extended to us.

Holding onto anger and unforgiveness, and allowing bitterness to emerge causes great psychological distress and will lead to depression or anxiety issues. Releasing anger and forgiving others helps us be whole in mind and body.

Why is God's anger different than ours?

> *Ye shall not afflict any widow, or fatherless child. If thou afflict them in any wise, and they cry at all unto me, I will surely hear their cry; And my wrath shall wax hot, and I will kill you with the sword, and your wives shall be widows, and your children fatherless.*
> (Exodus 22:22-24 KJV)

This is an example of what makes God angry. God does not like to see the weak of this world abused or taken advantage of. We, as mere humans, will often get angry with someone over trivial things but God reserves his anger for truly important things.

> *The wrath of God came upon them, and slew the fattest of them, and smote down the chosen men of Israel. For all this they sinned still, and believed not for his wondrous works. Therefore their days did he consume in vanity, and their years in trouble.*
> *When he slew them, then they sought him: and they returned and enquired early after God.*
> *And they remembered that God was their rock, and the high God their redeemer. Nevertheless they did flatter him with their mouth, and they lied unto him with their tongues.*
> *For their heart was not right with him, neither were they stedfast in his covenant. But he, being full of compassion, forgave their iniquity, and destroyed them not: yea, many a time turned he his anger away, and did not stir up all his wrath.*
> (Psalms 78:31-38 KJV)

God becomes angry with us when we continue to stray from the way He would have us to live. But He does restrain His anger because He does love us. He knows what is best for us, He tells us, and we continually refuse to listen. God will show His anger at us sometimes as a way of bringing us back to repentance.

> *And the LORD passed by before him, and proclaimed, The LORD, The LORD God, merciful and gracious, longsuffering, and abundant in goodness and truth,*
> *Keeping mercy for thousands, forgiving iniquity and transgression and sin, and that will by no means clear the guilty; visiting the iniquity of the fathers upon the children, and upon the children's children, unto the third and to the fourth generation.*
> (Exodus 34:6-7 KJV)

God's anger is always tempered with love. As we see, He restrains his anger but if we continue to do wrong we will eventually be punished, but that is for our own good. God treats us as our fathers should. He punishes us out of love without staying angry with us.

It is God's place alone to exact vengeance on someone. God's wrath is always justified and good, but our wrath on others is always misplaced and wrong. Only God is righteous enough to make a proper judgment as to who is deserving of His wrath and who is not.

> *Dearly beloved, avenge not yourselves, but rather give place unto wrath: for it is written, Vengeance is mine; I will repay, saith the Lord. Therefore if thine*

> *enemy hunger, feed him; if he thirst, give him drink: for in so doing thou shalt heap coals of fire on his head. Be not overcome of evil, but overcome evil with good.*
> (Romans 12:19-21 KJV)

Jesus only became angry and took action for a proper reason. If we are to become angry at all it should at least be for a Godly reason, such as in this incident when people were doing something so contrary to God's Word.

> *And Jesus went into the temple of God, and cast out all them that sold and bought in the temple, and overthrew the tables of the moneychangers, and the seats of them that sold doves,*
> (Matthew 21:12 KJV)

> *And he saith unto them, Is it lawful to do good on the sabbath days, or to do evil? to save life, or to kill? But they held their peace.*
> *And when he had looked round about on them with anger, being grieved for the hardness of their hearts, he saith unto the man, Stretch forth thine hand. And he stretched it out: and his hand was restored whole as the other.*
> (Mark 3:4-5 KJV)

Jesus was angry with the stubborn leaders, and instead of doing something to punish them, He did something constructive with His anger so that they might change their way of thinking. We need to do the same when we are angry with someone. We need to channel our anger in a positive way in hopes of affecting a change in that person.

In Sum:

We are to avoid patterns of self-oriented thought that result in anger. If we do let anger fester and take control of us it will eventually lead us into other sins and subsequently will lead us away from God. If we do become angry it should be for a Godly reason and not out of pride or some other earthly reason. We should only become angry at evil (when someone breaks a law or a command of God's). But our reaction should always be out of love; we should look for a way to temper our anger so that no confrontation results. If we were truly motivated by God we would want that person to change their ways.

We should never wish to take vengeance on someone ourselves. As we saw in the above scriptures, only God is righteous enough to judge mankind and exact his wrath on those who deserve it. Everything God does is ultimately for the good of all mankind. When we counsel others we need to tell them to strive to have Godly anger while avoiding the mistake of believing that we are in the position of responding with Godly wrath.

The Psycho-Emotional State of Love

He that loveth not knoweth not God; for <u>God is love</u>.
(1 John 4:8 KJV)

One of the most confusing words in the English language is the word love. Asking individuals what it means will provide as many definitions as individuals that are asked. Yet, that psycho-emotional state has a profound impact on our psychology and the level of joy that we find in our existence. Because we are made in God's image, then our very nature should be love. Unfortunately because of the fallen nature in each one of us, the Word and Spirit of God must renew this aspect of our psychology. We love God because He first Loved us.

The statement that "God is love" is a very complete description of the term love, but requires that the individual truly know who God is and therefore, have a deep understanding of His Word.

The Greek language has three common terms that are used for love:

Greek term	Meaning
agapē	self-sacrificing or benevolence
phileō	to be a friend to
eros	desire or physiological love

Each one of these terms has a spiritual, cognitive (thinking), behavioral, and emotional component. For example: The spiritual element in agapē love is the Spirit of God, and this is found in the self-sacrificial nature of Jesus' death on the cross for our sins.

Greater love hath no man than this, that a man lay down his life for his friends. (John 15:13 KJV)

Without the Spirit of God this level of self-sacrifice is rarely found. The cognitive element of agapē love is seen when the thoughts we have toward others is that they are more important than we are. These thoughts require that we recognize that all others are made in the image of God, as we are, and therefore, we are to care for their needs first before our own.

For God so loved the world that <u>He gave His only begotten Son</u>, that whosoever believeth in Him should not perish, but have everlasting life.
(John 3:16 KJV)

The third element or behaviors of agapē love indicates a need for action.

Herein perceive we the love of God, because <u>He laid down His life</u> for us: and we ought to lay down our lives for the brethren. (1 John 3:16 KJV)

These actions stem from the choices that are made in the thought element of love. Without the spirit and thoughts there are seldom actions.

The fourth element of agapē love, the emotion, only comes when all of the other three elements are in process.

<u>Who for the joy</u> that was set before Him endured the cross, despising the shame, and is set down at the right hand of the throne of God.
(Hebrews 12:2b KJV)

This is frequently the element that individuals demand be present first before they will choose the thoughts and behaviors. Frequently in troubled marriages individuals will claim that they do not feel in love with their spouse. Unfortunately this is a result of the choice to stop the loving thoughts and behaviors that would result in the warm fuzzy feelings associated with love.

Our psychological health is personified by knowledge of God's agapē love for us. This truth needs to be known and meditated upon to free us from the satanic lie of rejection that leads to pain and destruction.

> *The thief cometh not but for to steal, and to kill, and to destroy: I am come that they might have life, and that they might have it more abundantly.* (John 10:10 KJV)

One of satan's goals in our lives is to stop love. He has come to steal, kill and destroy the love that should be dominating our lives, and replace it with rejection and hate (the next subject).

The loving attitude and behavior that we are to exhibit toward one another is found in many places in the Bible, but none so clearly as in 1 Corinthians 13. Here we see a list of thoughts, behaviors and attitudes that challenge each one of us to die to the self for the good of others.

> *Love is patient and kind. Love is not jealous or boastful or proud or rude. It does not demand its own way. It is not irritable, and it keeps no record of being wronged. It does not rejoice about injustice but rejoices whenever the truth wins out. Love never gives up, never loses faith, is always hopeful, and endures through every circumstance. Prophecy and speaking in unknown languages and special knowledge will become useless. But love will last forever!*
> (1 Corinthians 13: 4-7 NLT)

In Sum:

Our psychological well-being is based upon God's love for us. We are instructed to demonstrate that love for each other, and this contributes to our psychological health. All three forms of love are from God. All good things come down from Him. Love is about the acceptance we experience. God's acceptance of us is completed in Jesus Christ. The core issue in our lives can be our failure to accept others or be accepted by others. This rejection or withholding of love causes psychological distress that can lead to emotional issues like depression and anxiety. The withholding of love to others is a violation of God's command to love your neighbor as yourself. This sin causes pain and suffering in our lives. Further, being made in God's image, and He is love, we reject our Creator and ourselves in the process.

> *Beloved, now we are the sons of God, and it doth not yet appear what we shall be: but we know that, when He shall appear, we shall be like Him; for we shall see Him as He is.*
> (1 John 3:2 KJV)

> *Beloved, let us love one another: for love is of God; and everyone that loveth is born of God, and knoweth God. He that loveth not knoweth not God; for God is love.*
> (1 John 4:7-8 KJV)

The Psycho-Emotional State of Hate

The fear of the LORD is to hate evil: pride, and arrogancy, and the evil way, and the forward mouth, do I hate.
(Proverbs 8:13 KJV)

Hate is commanded by God as an attitude and response that we are to express toward the things that God hates. We are not to hate other individuals, because they are made in God's image, and to hate them would amount to hating the image of God. We are to hate the evil that men do. We hate because God hates. This is another characteristic from being made in God's image. Our psychology needs to hate just as God's psychology does. We can only correctly hate by knowing God and what He hates.

But this thou hast, that thou hatest the deeds of the Nicolaitanes, which I also hate. (Revelation 2:6 KJV)

The hating of evil is one of the most important actions that we can do to keep our psychology healthy and Christ like. To hate evil is to push it away and reject it. We are told to hate what is evil and love what is good (Rom 12:9). Rejecting evil keeps us from looking upon it or allowing it into our lives. Evil is like a virus, you must make contact with it for it to infect you.

Abstain from all appearance of evil.
(1 Thessalonians 5:22 KJV)

Hating what is evil will prevent the contact with it, and the subsequent sin that may follow. It will help keep your mind free from the bondage of evil and sin.

Jesus Christ was hated by the world, and we are told that the world will hate us.

If the world hate you, ye know that it hated me before it hated you.
John 15:18 (GW)

This hate is painful, and hate led to the crucifixion of our Lord Jesus Christ. We are told to take up our cross and follow Him.

Then Jesus said unto his disciples, If any man will come after me, let him deny himself, and take up his cross, and follow me. (Matthew 16:24 KJV)

This implies experiencing the rejection of the world around us.

Blessed are ye, when men shall hate you, and when they shall separate you from their company, and shall reproach you, and cast out your name as evil, for the Son of man's sake. (Luke 6:22 KJV)

When the world rejects us we have joined in the suffering of Christ. When our family hates us it hurts. Mental anguish is experienced when we are rejected. Frequently when the ones that we love reject us, the result is depression (discussed in detail later in the text). The act of hating another believer will cause serious mental and emotional problems in an individual.

But he that hateth his brother is in darkness, and walketh in darkness, and knoweth not whither he goeth, because that darkness hath blinded his eyes. (1 John 2:11 KJV)

In Sum:

God alone knows what is good and bad for us. We are to hate what He hates and love what He loves. To violate this simple rule causes sin and suffering to enter our and others' lives. Hate is an action of will with corresponding behaviors to reject. To reject what God loves (man) and has died for will make you sick in mind and heart. The health of our psychology requires Godly hate to keep our mind free from the bondage of sin.

Be ye therefore followers of God, as dear children. (Ephesians 5:1 KJV)

The Psycho-Emotional State of Humility

Likewise, ye younger, submit yourselves unto the elder. Yea, all of you be subject one to another, and be clothed with humility: for God resisteth the proud, and giveth grace to the humble. Humble yourselves therefore under the mighty hand of God, that he may exalt you in due time.
(1 Peter 5:5-6 KJV)

To be humble is to actively live knowing that you are not God. Being humble frees us from the impossible burden of trying to be a god. It takes a tremendous amount of psychological resources to keep projecting the lie that you are "somebody" or are more important than others. This waste of mental energy can leave the individual in confusion and exhausted. Being humble, on the other hand, lets God be God and by the power of His might He will exalt you.

Take my yoke upon you, and learn of me, for I am meek and lowly in heart: and ye shall find rest unto your souls, For my yoke is easy and my burden is light.
(Matthew 11:29-30 KJV)

The psychological state of humility is from Jesus Christ. Our fallen nature is prideful and opposes humility. We are commanded to be humble like Jesus so that we may find rest in our lives. Humility is an attitude we are to possess as children of God.

Whosoever therefore shall humble himself as this little child, the same is greatest in the kingdom of heaven.
(Matthew 18:4 KJV)

It is a lie to think that it is difficult to be humble. The truth is that it is difficult for us when we choose not to be humble.

For whosoever exalteth himself shall be abased; and he that humbleth himself shall be exalted.
(Luke 14:11 KJV)

Only by renewing our mind through washing with the Word can we demonstrate Christ-like humility. Our psychology needs the repair work from God's Spirit to keep us humble and at rest.

In Sum:

Humility is an attitude of recognizing our place as servants at the bottom, not the top. It is emotionally draining to keep trying to be what we are not. The entire world wants to be a god. We as believers in Christ Jesus know who our God is, and we are not Him. We do not have to worry about our position because God's plan is that we be with Him in the high place of heaven.

For thus saith the high and lofty One that inhabiteth eternity, whose name is Holy; I dwell in the high and holy place, with him also that is of a contrite and humble spirit, to revive the spirit of the humble, and to revive the heart of the contrite ones.
(Isaiah 57:15 KJV)

Biblical Psychology

The Psycho-Emotional State of Pride

For all that is in the world, the lust of the flesh, and the lust of the eyes, and the pride of life, is not of the Father, but is of the world
(1 John 2:16 KJV)

The pride of life is not of the Father, it is of our fallen nature and the cause of satan's ejection from heaven. God has no need for pride. He is the Creator of all and is exalted by all of creation. Man has fallen from his natural place with God, and tries to use pride to regain that place. Our position is secure in Jesus. To develop pride in our own lives and accomplishments denies the Father's hand in our lives. Our psychology is corrupted by pride.

Pride goeth before destruction, and an haughty spirit before a fall.
(Proverbs 16:18 KJV)

A man's pride shall bring him low: but honor shall uphold the humble in spirit. (Proverbs 29:23 KJV)

The pride that we hold in ourselves is the pride of life. Believing that we are something other than a child of God corrupts us. Yet, child of God is the highest place that can be obtained. When we are not satisfied with our high servant position then we seek God's job. This will kill an individual, physically and spiritually.

The stress of pride eats away at the mind and thoughts and steals the peace of God from the life of man. Stress causes the mind to become stupid and slow. Few things in life damage our psychology like the stress that is induced by pride. Pride results in a mind that is deceived and unable to see the truth. What we believe in has become a lie and we are blind to reality.

The pride of thine heart hath deceived thee, thou that dwellest in the clefts of the rock, whose habitation is high; that saith in his heart, Who shall bring me down to the ground? Though thou exalt thyself as the eagle, and though thou set thy nest among the stars, thence will I bring thee down, saith the LORD. (Obadiah 1:3-4 KJV)

It is God in us that provides all of our standing in life, not we ourselves. We are His children and the sheep of His pasture. He made us, owns us, and all the pastures of life. We are but dust without Him.

The strife that we have with others is from pride.

Only by pride cometh contention: but with the well advised is wisdom.
(Proverbs 13:10 KJV)

When pride enters our psychology we can never lose an argument or fight. We must be ready to defend our high position of being a god. Constant striving and contention is emotionally and psychologically destructive. We become weak and fall into sickness and despair.

In Sum:

Pride is not for us. God is God and is exalted by His very existence. Pride is our false attempts to be what we are not. Pride will destroy our lives and negatively impact those around us. It is perhaps more contagious than all of the other sins that are chosen by man. Focusing upon humility leads to the destruction of pride. Who we are in Christ Jesus is all that we are.

The Psycho-Emotional State of Peace

Man has long desired peace, but found it to be elusive because, on his own, he does not know how to acquire it. In the Old Testament peace indicated material prosperity or physical safety. But for the New Testament church peace means far more: spiritual well-being, completeness and stability of the mind.

Finally, brethren, farewell. Be perfect, be of good comfort, be of one mind, live in peace; and the God of love and peace shall be with you. (2 Corinthians 13:11 KJV)

True, heartfelt peace is not merely the absence of or restraint from anger and conflict, but a positive, proactive, heartfelt peace of yielding to God and of good will toward all. This is a psychological state marked by the absence of tension; a calmness that is punctuated by the fruit of the Spirit.

But the fruit of the Spirit is love, joy, peace, longsuffering, gentleness, goodness, faith, meekness, temperance: against such there is no law. (Galatians 5:22-23 KJV)

Because peace is so sought after, individuals may not make wise decisions about motivations others have behind peace. Can we trust just anyone who wants peace?

Draw me not away with the wicked, and with the workers of iniquity, which speak peace to their neighbors, but mischief is in their hearts. (Psalms 28:3 KJV)

Because, even because they have seduced my people, saying, Peace; and there was no peace; and one built up a wall, and, lo, others daubed it with untempered mortar. (Ezekiel 13:10 KJV)

Thus saith the LORD concerning the prophets that make my people err, that bite with their teeth, and cry, Peace; and he that putteth not into their mouths, they even prepare war against him. (Micah 3:5 KJV)

For when they shall say, Peace and safety; then sudden destruction cometh upon them, as travail upon a woman with child; and they shall not escape. (1 Thessalonians 5:3 KJV)

Can the wicked have peace?

The wicked man travaileth with pain all his days, and the number of years is hidden to the oppressor. A dreadful sound is in his ears: in prosperity the destroyer shall come upon him. (Job 15:20-21 KJV)

There is no peace, saith the LORD, unto the wicked. (Isaiah 48:22 KJV)

There can be no peace between a man who is involved with sin and God. The peace that the mind craves goes when obedience to God is abandoned. The world does not recognize true peace. During man's entire history there have been only a very few years of global peace. The leaders and false prophets lie to the people, "saying, 'Peace, peace!' when there is no peace."

They have healed also the hurt of the daughter of my people slightly, saying, Peace, peace; when there is no peace. (Jeremiah 6:14 KJV)

Peace is perhaps the perfect state of mind. The Bible tells us that God has called His saints to be at peace.

If it be possible, as much as lieth in you, live peaceably with all men. (Romans 12:18 KJV)

> *But if the unbelieving depart, let him depart. A brother or a sister is not under bondage in such cases: but God hath called us to peace.*
> (1 Corinthians 7:15 KJV)

> *And let the peace of God rule in your hearts, to the which also ye are called in one body; and be ye thankful.* (Colossians 3:15 KJV)

> *Follow peace with all men, and holiness, without which no man shall see the Lord.* (Hebrews 12:14 KJV)

The peace from God that is the focus of our desire comes only when we choose to be obedient to Him. This requires a humble response to God's commands.

> *Great peace have they which love thy law: and nothing shall offend them. LORD, I have hoped for thy salvation, and done thy commandments.*
> (Psalms 119:165-166 KJV)

> *O that thou hadst hearkened to my commandments! then had thy peace been as a river, and thy righteousness as the waves of the sea.* (Isaiah 48:18 KJV)

God has called us to peace. He expects us to keep His commandments, and in return He gives us peace of mind.

> *When a man's ways please the LORD, he maketh even his enemies to be at peace with him.* (Proverbs 16:7 KJV)

Sin separates man from God, causing a confrontational relationship with Him whereby man receives the wrath of God. This is anything but peaceful! Peace leads to more peace, washing away strife and fear as a river sweeps away debris. God grants peace as a gift through Jesus Christ.

> *The word which God sent unto the children of Israel, preaching peace by Jesus Christ (who is Lord of all).*
> (Acts 10:36 KJV)

> *Therefore being justified by faith, we have peace with God through our Lord Jesus Christ.* (Romans 5:1 KJV)

> *For it pleased the Father that in him should all fulness dwell; And, having made peace through the blood of his cross, by him to reconcile all things unto himself; by him, I say, whether they be things in earth, or things in heaven.* (Colossians 1:19-20 KJV)

> *Now the Lord of peace himself give you peace always by all means.*
> (2 Thessalonians 3:16 KJV)

We have peace through the blood He shed on the cross. The suffering and sacrifice of Jesus Christ in life and death has opened the way for peace between man and God and between man and man.
The peace with God brought about by Christ Jesus brings us healing.

> *But he was wounded for our transgressions, he was bruised for our iniquities: the chastisement of our peace was upon him; and with his stripes we are healed.*
> (Isaiah 53:5 KJV)

God's peace and unity are states of mind that promote each other.

> *For he is our peace, who hath made both one, and hath broken down the middle wall of partition between us; Having abolished in his flesh the enmity, even the law of commandments contained in ordinances; for to make in himself of twain one new man, so making peace; And that he might reconcile both unto God in one body by the cross, having slain the enmity thereby: And came and preached peace to you which were afar off, and to them that were nigh.*
> (Ephesians 2:14-17 KJV)

What kind of heart or attitude is required in order to have peace?

Be careful for nothing; but in every thing by prayer and supplication with thanksgiving let your requests be made known unto God. And the peace of God, which passeth all understanding, shall keep your hearts and minds through Christ Jesus. Finally, brethren, whatsoever things are true, whatsoever things are honest, whatsoever things are just, whatsoever things are pure, whatsoever things are lovely, whatsoever things are of good report; if there be any virtue, and if there be any praise, think on these things. Those things, which ye have both learned, and received, and heard, and seen in me, do: and the God of peace shall be with you.
(Philippians 4:6-9 KJV)

Peace I leave with you, my peace I give unto you: not as the world giveth, give I unto you. Let not your heart be troubled, neither let it be afraid. (John 14:27 KJV)

God gives His peace to those of a pure or righteous heart and mind. The transition from Old to New Testament usage of "peace" strikingly illustrates its personal, internal application: Out of about 90 New Testament instances, 90% refer to *heartfelt peace*. The internalized, heartfelt peace is unhindered by the world's strife.

These things I have spoken unto you, that in me ye might have peace. In the world ye shall have tribulation: but be of good cheer; I have overcome the world.
(John 16:33 KJV)

For to be carnally minded is death; but to be spiritually minded is life and peace. Because the carnal mind is enmity against God: for it is not subject to the law of God, neither indeed can be. So then they that are in the flesh cannot please God.
(Romans 8:6-8 KJV)

God's peace is a deep, spiritual peace unaffected by the world. We can have this peace, if we truly trust in God's redemptive plan for mankind. We must be striving to produce His character and choose to be obedient to His Word. This is a righteous mind set.

And the work of righteousness shall be peace; and the effect of righteousness quietness and assurance for ever. And my people shall dwell in a peaceable habitation, and in sure dwellings, and in quiet resting places.
(Isaiah 32:17-18 KJV)

But the wisdom that is from above is first pure, then peaceable, gentle, and easy to be intreated, full of mercy and good fruits, without partiality, and without hypocrisy. And the fruit of righteousness is sown in peace of them that make peace. (James 3:17-18 KJV)

Righteousness produces peace with its qualities of quietness and assurance, but at the same time, peace provides the proper environment for righteousness to grow. One builds upon the other. A home without peace hinders the development of righteousness. Thus, God allows a Christian to divorce an abusive, unconverted mate that chooses to leave.

But if the unbelieving depart, let him depart. A brother or a sister is not under bondage in such cases: but God hath called us to peace.
(1 Corinthians 7:15 KJV)

Peace does not just happen, it requires a real effort on our part. Our fallen nature wants to do the very thing to block God's peace. We need to know that seeking God is the path to peace.

Depart from evil, and do good; seek peace, and pursue it. The eyes of the LORD are upon the righteous, and his ears are open unto their cry.
(Psalms 34:14-15 KJV)

But glory, honour, and peace, to every man that worketh good, to the Jew first, and also to the Gentile:

For there is no respect of persons with God. (Romans 2:10-11 KJV)

Let us therefore follow after the things which make for peace, and things wherewith one may edify another. (Romans 14:19 KJV)

Wherefore, beloved, seeing that ye look for such things, be diligent that ye may be found of him in peace, without spot, and blameless. (2 Peter 3:14 KJV)

Making peace with God and man takes real effort! Although a gift from God through Christ, peace has to be sought. The pursuit of peace is not merely an elimination of discord, but peace is produced by conscious mental effort to overcome the evil in our lives while asking God to grant us peace. As Biblical counselors we should encourage everyone to seek God's peace. We also need to remind them that by themselves, however, their efforts to achieve peace are not enough. Jesus Christ Himself will ultimately bring peace to all mankind.

For unto us a child is born, unto us a son is given: and the government shall be upon his shoulder: and his name shall be called Wonderful, Counsellor, The mighty God, The everlasting Father, <u>The Prince of Peace.</u> (Isaiah 9:6 KJV)

Depressive State of Mind

The first common issue that will be discussed is depression. There are numerous places in the Bible where individuals have developed a depressive state of mind.

> *For we would not, brethren, have you ignorant of our trouble which came to us in Asia, that we were pressed out of measure, above strength insomuch that we despaired even of life: But we had the sentence of death in ourselves, that we should not trust in ourselves, but in God which raiseth the dead.*
> (2 Corinthians 1:8-9 KJV)

Most of the time a person's choices are the root cause of a depressive state of mind. Therefore it is the correct choices that most often result in the depression leaving. There are four common ways to develop this mood problem. You can make a series of mistakes that cause your life to fall apart, someone else can make choices that impact you so that you cannot stand up under the stress, physical illness occurring in you or someone close to you results in stress and depression, you are under direct demonic attack (you must be causing satan some grief). As stated earlier, it is all sin-based.

Depression can be brief and mild, or long standing and severe. Sometimes we use the terms "feeling low" to describe a depressive state. Temporary low feelings are common to us all and of little concern. Many things in this life can leave us in the "blues" for a while. This may simply be an appropriate response to being in the world but not of this world. A truly depressive state in a mild form can be described as feeling low consistently for three to four weeks. Most of the time we have hope and faith in God as well as the love and support of family and the church to help us through a mild depressive state if it should arise in our life. For example: The death of a loved-one is a common trigger of a mild depressive episode that can last a few months.

No matter how it starts, depression can quickly become a physiological condition. A chemical shortage in the brain makes it nearly impossible for a seriously depressed individual to come out of it without help. God can and will heal some people instantly (He is willing). Once it has become physical, the depression issue is the same concern as all other medical issues (cancer or any physical illness). It is physical, and professional medical help <u>may</u> be required. The use of most forms of secular psychology may actually cause the depression to become worse. The family doctor and a Christian counselor or pastor can be very effective in helping. Do not think that you as a compassionate minister or lay counselor can fix everything (only God can do this). Pray and listen to the wisdom of the Holy Spirit.

All levels of depression can be identified by a symptom list. This list is based on statistics that have been collected that describe the common issues that depressed people report. It is simply *reported facts*.

Clarification:

One of the more common beliefs in the Church today is that there is always something demonic happening when depression is present. It is true that it is always important to evaluate the spiritual battleground when ministering to anyone about anything. Yet, while demonic oppression may be the cause of a depressive state, it is seldom directly involved. Nevertheless, spiritual oppression should be considered to be involved until it is taken care of and ruled out. Christians have the authority to cast out all demonic spiritual forces (Luke 10:17-19), and should pray to do so always when ministering to those suffering with depression.

Symptoms of Depression

    A.   Affect: An individual's mood has changed significantly during the past four or five weeks. There are persistent periods during the day where the person's feelings are of:

- Sadness
- Discouragement
- Hopelessness
- Irritability
- Crying
- Helplessness

    B.   Behavior: Behavioral changes are apparent. These may include:

- Fatigue
- Sleep disturbances—insomnia, early-morning awakening, or oversleeping
- Increase or loss of appetite
- Weight gain or weight loss
- Psychomotor retardation—feeling "slowed down"

    C.   Cognition: Depression impacts thinking. A person may have trouble with the following:

- Difficulty concentrating
- Difficulty making decisions
- Negative thought patterns about self, the world, and the future. Negative thoughts about the self may take the form of, "I'm a loser." Negative thoughts about the world might be, "Everything is awful." When thinking about the future, negative self-talk might be reflected in the statement, "Everything is going to stay bad."

There are many common causes of an individual developing a persistent depressive state. The list below is not exhaustive or indicating that a depressive state must occur if one or more of these situations are present.

Common Causes of Depression

    A.   Loss issues

- Death of a loved one
- Friendship breakup or change
- Losing face or loss of accurate self-image
- Several lifestyle changes or transitions

    B.   Prolonged stress

- Too many things to do each day
- Pressure at home or at work
- Captivity or prisoner of war
- Extended abuse or rejection

C. Body chemistry;

Research has indicated that some depressions can be the result of a chemical imbalance in the brain. These may be the result of natural body changes or ingestion (food, drink…)

D. Physical causes

- Life events such as illness may be linked to depression (heart attack survivors)
- Hormonal deficiencies have been noted to influence mood and overall functioning

E. Faulty thinking

- Faulty or inaccurate self-talk
- Irrational, distorted thinking

Spiritual Causes:

- Oppression: Satan's attacks because you are serving the Kingdom.
- Unbelief: Jesus is not sufficient enough to forgive my sins.
- Ignorance of the Word: Give praise to God only when you feel like praising or things are going good.
- Lack of a growing relationship with Christ: Isn't Sunday church enough?
- Sin/Pride: I can do what I want. / You don't need anyone.
- Belief that God has abandoned you.

Once a persistent depressive state has developed in an individual's life there are many levels of intervention that may be used depending upon how much their ability to function in day-to-day life has deteriorated.

Intervention

A. The physiological triad: A physical intervention for healthy brain chemistry that should always be part of life.

- Sleep: promote consistent structured sleeping (8 hours)
- Eating: regular balanced healthy meals
- Exercise: gentle walking or other regular light physical activity.

B. The Cognitive triad: Dispute satan's lying message about the condition and life.

- You are hopeless (no matter how much you try).
- You are not acceptable (no one would love you as you are).
- There is no hope for the future (give up!).

C. Reduce the stress

- Make a list of what must be done and what can be set aside.
- If situations are changeable, change them.
- Ask for help
- Take care of your needs (frequent breaks, take relaxing hot bubble baths).

D. Medication (seldom necessary)

- If they state that they want to die and have a plan.
- If they can't function well enough to work out of it.
- If they can't back away from the stress.

Depression Part II: Detailed Intervention Strategies.

Because depression is so common in life it is important to have an understanding of how to help ourselves and others.

Dealing with Wounded Narcissism & Self-Orientation:

Depression typically involves the development of an *unhealthy focus on the self*. Discerning how the depression begins, or the specific stressors that may be involved, is helpful when you are trying to help the person avoid future depressive episodes. But, regardless of the origin of the depression, the end product involves an individual who thinks mostly of him or her self. If the person is thinking of harming themselves or others, get professional help (law enforcement and/or medical) and call your pastor immediately.

Wounded Narcissism is a term that describes the depressed person's compulsive preoccupation with the pain and suffering that has arisen from being psychologically, emotionally, or spiritually wounded.

Some of the ways that wounded narcissism may be observed are found in the statements that the individual makes about themselves:

- My pain
- My suffering
- My loss
- My …….

Because they own or possess the wound, it may be hard for them to let go of it (it belongs to them). This seems confusing because it is the suffering that they want to stop. Yet, in deeper depressions the fixation on the pain is all that the person believes that they have left. They may even state that they have become the pain.

Self-Orientation is a term that implies a general preoccupation with the self, to the detriment of relationships with man and God. This may include wounded narcissism, but may also be self-chosen, not the result of the emotional injury. Pride can often be found behind the thinking that "I should never have any problems… why does God allow this?"

Ways that the self-orientation may be observed:

- self-loathing
- self-hate
- self-pity
- self-anger
- self- …..

If they believe that they have made a mistake, this helps them to self-punish and denies the *Grace of God* (Galatians 2:21). Inaccurate and falsely low self-image is pride's best friend. They will state that they are prideful of their efforts to measure up and get life right.

The *Intervention* for the self-orientation involves helping them to see that they have the focus on themselves and then encouraging them to turn the focus back on God and others. As long as they place themselves and their pain in the center of the universe, there will be little use for God, and their fellow man will only be something that can be used.

Action steps to take:

After developing a clear understanding of the source and depth of the depressive state, you may respond to them,

> "I see that you are really hurting about the way you were treated…
>
> you must be getting tired of the pain…. maybe it is time for it to stop." (apply this to yourself if it is you with the issue)

This demonstrates *empathy, understanding, and a suggestion toward change*. Help them to understand that emotional pain is a part of the condition of depression. If a person gets a scratch on their leg, they do not become a scratch. Likewise, if they have a depressive state, they have not become the depressive pain. It is just part of being temporarily sick.

Always suggest that the person should do something for someone else (Philippians 2:4). This takes the focus off of them and places it on others. It produces a *Jesus perspective and priorities.* Help them to remember that *God is the center of the universe…* not them and their pain. The truth is, if all we thought about is ourselves then we should all be depressed. Our hope is to be in the Lord (Psalm 25:5).

If they have been persisting in the self-oriented behavior, *help them to see how they benefit from it* and then help them to discover other ways to get those needs met. For example,

> *"I see that others have demonstrated concern and attention toward you during your depression… do you think that you can get this level of interaction from others without the depression?"*

Dealing with Anger at others:

A loved one who has died, an employer who is harsh, a relationship falling apart, or any other *stressor involving the behavior or implied behavior of another that is seen as the cause of injury* (to body, mind, or spirit) can result in intense anger leading to a depressive state.

<u>Depressive Anger</u> is an outward or inward directed reaction to some form of perceived wounding. The person who does not turn inward on their pain will express anger outward. Others may see them as always angry or hateful.

The anger needs to be placed at the foot of the Cross, under the guidelines of the Word and the Holy Spirit. The anger may have been "justified" at the beginning of the depression, but as the Bible tells us it must be placed in God's hands.

<u>Forgiveness</u> is a divine process and very healing. If persistent anger is a problem it is important to remind the individual how much Jesus has forgiven them (Ephesians 4:32). Also, the act of forgiveness will help them to heal from their injuries. If the outside stress is from persecution directed toward their faith, then they need to be encouraged to pray for the persecutors to be blessed (Matthew 5:44).

To intervene in the anger:

- ✓ Allow them to express it appropriately (this means talking—not violence).
- ✓ Try to learn and understand who or what the object of the anger is and why.
- ✓ Help them recognize that being angry is a choice of their own, not a choice of the object or person of their anger.
- ✓ Remind them that staying angry keeps them under the control of others; it is bondage to something or someone.
- ✓ Tell them that the anger is a response not a solution.

Styles of Depressive Thought

There are a number of styles of maladaptive thinking that are found in depression. Each one contributes to holding the person in the depressive state of mind.

<u>Black and white or dichotomous thinking</u> involves believing that if elements of life are not perfect then they are the worst. There is no gray area in their thinking. Because feelings are a product of our thoughts, this leads individuals to be down because being perfect is an attribute of God not man. They do not experience normal life.

<u>Catastrophic thinking</u> results in believing the absolute worst possible thought about a situation or event. The individual persistently looks for only the bad in most situations, and makes everything out to be worse than it is. In conjunction with black and white thinking, catastrophic thought can lead to fear, anxiety and a serious depressive mood.

<u>Selective abstraction</u> is a style of thinking that keeps a person focusing on the sadness even though there is a lot to be happy about. Counting their blessings is forgotten or not even viewed as possible (I Thessalonians 5:18). They selectively reject all good reports in favor of their pain or negative mood.

These styles of thought can be part of the character of an individual that result in frequent and life-long depression, or they may emerge during the neural physiological disturbance in the brain that is found in serious depression. Intervention requires helping them to see that the style of thought is counter-productive to recovery (use the reality in the Word of God (Hebrews 4:12) to expose the maladaptive thoughts). They need to be told directly that they are believing a lie of satan and rejecting God's truth.

Intervention Summary:

- Evaluate and change the condition of the physiological triad (eating, sleeping and exercise). Help them to structure and schedule their life.
- Contradict the psychological triad (lies of satan). Use the Bible.
- Assess the level of self-involvement and give an assignment to help someone else.
- Listen to the anger, then provide understanding, perspective and coaching for prayer.
- Identify maladaptive thought patterns and discuss how they keep a person depressed.

In Sum:

As with all of life's issues, in dealing with a persistent depressive state, it is important to keep in mind that Jesus is the ultimate answer. If the person does not know Jesus Christ as Lord and Savior, they will only experience temporary relief from your ministry and counsel. When a person is so severely depressed that they cannot function or listen to you, then they must be given immediate medical help. Remember that regardless how it starts, serious depression is a physical problem.

Biblical Psychology

Anxious States of Mind

Anxiety is a very common problem that we all may face. We are encouraged to be anxious for nothing. Yet, we are often anxious about every little thing. There seems to be an increase in anxiety that is present today, even within the church:

> *Men's hearts failing them for fear, and for looking after those things which are coming on the earth: for the powers of heaven shall be shaken.*
>
> (Luke 21:26 KJV)

We all have had the experience of feeling nervous about something sometime in our lives. Persistent anxiety states are not about feeling a little nervous about something. These high levels of anxiety leave the individual focusing on fear to the extent that they are not functioning correctly in their daily lives. The Bible states that "true love casts out all fear" so why is it that Christians have so much fear and anxiety? As mentioned previously, we are in a sin-filled world, and none of us is free from its effects. Even common anxious feelings can be helped by the understanding and interventions presented in this chapter.

Anxiety Symptoms:

The principle component of all anxiety states is fear. This fear may become a serious problem in life when:

- It stops normal mental functioning
- Prevents a person from doing normal activities
- Results in physical issues like high blood pressure
- Causes relationship issues
- Cannot be stopped by the person who is fearful

Symptoms that are visible include:

- Rapid breathing or hyperventilation
- Dizziness and confusion
- Avoiding situations without a reasonable explanation
- Excessive sweating and skin flushing
- Shaking and drooling
- Collapse and loss of consciousness
- Withdrawal and isolation
- Flashbacks and hallucinations

Note: While some of these symptoms seem to represent more serious forms of anxiety, many of them can be found to some degree in everyone who has developed any level of anxiety problem.

The question that needs to be answered to separate common passing anxiety experiences from persistent anxiety states is:

How does it happen?

Choosing to Develop an Anxiety Problem: Open worry and/or weeping

- Mind: Making the choice not to believe God
- Body: Choosing physical chaos over physical discipline
- Spirit: Choosing sin, listening to satan's lies

Making decisions that reflect disbelief

Choosing to be anxious for anything and everything, particularly the future can quickly develop into a persistent anxiety issue.

> *But seek ye first the kingdom of God, and his righteousness; and all these things shall be added unto you. Take therefore no thought for the morrow: for the morrow shall take thought for the things of itself. Sufficient unto the day is the evil thereof.*
> (Matthew 6:33-34 KJV)

Choosing not to believe or not knowing that God loves you, and will strengthen you and help you, can result in the thoughts that you are all alone.

> *Fear thou not; for I am with thee: be not dismayed; for I am thy God: I will strengthen thee; yea, I will help thee; yea, I will uphold thee with the right hand of my righteousness.*
> (Isaiah 41:10 KJV)

Choosing to be the Lone Ranger

No accountability in life leaves an individual to self-govern. This is known as anarchy. We are never to go it alone because we are part of the Body of Christ. Each part is important to all of the others. No individual is to be functioning as an isolated church unto themselves.

> *For if they fall, the one will lift up his fellow: but woe to him that is alone when he falleth; for he hath not another to help him up.*
> (Ecclesiastes 4:10 KJV)

> *Choosing to be isolated and alone should make us develop anxiety!*

Without a prayer life there is no integrity. Without integrity an individual is open to all forms of spiritual attack. Going it alone indicates that the individual does not communicate with God in any real meaningful way. How is it that one can say that Jesus is in them and never talk to Him? The truth is that we are nothing but dirt without Jesus Christ. In this isolated state of mind anxiety cannot be far off.

Choosing physical chaos over physical discipline:

Failure to take care of the gift that God has given us will result in many problems. Anxiety is common among them. Our bodies are made to be in balance and God tells us that we are to be good stewards of that which we have been given. Common starting points for persistent anxiety states that arise out of our physical nature are:

- Choosing not to sleep enough
- Choosing not to eat properly
- Choosing not to exercise
- Choosing stressful situations
- Choosing to ignore your fatigue

> *Or do you not know that your body is the temple of the Holy Spirit who is in you, whom you have from God, and you are not your own? For you*

were bought at a price; therefore glorify God in your body and in your spirit, which are God's.
(1 Cor. 6:19-20 NKJV)
(See also: Hebrews 12:1-2, Luke 21:34, Proverbs 25:28)

Choosing to rebel has a price:

When we choose to sin against God and do what ought not to be done we will face consequences for our actions.

It is a fearful thing to fall into the hands of the living God.
(Hebrews 10:31 KJV)

This scripture indicates that to willfully sin <u>should</u> result in anxiety and fear. Satan wants to deceive us as he did Eve:

- He didn't say you would die (Genesis 3:4)
- My God is good and wants me to be happy
- Saying God is the cause
  The truth is that God does not cause evil or tempt us.
- Dwelling on the sinful message

Let no man say when he is tempted, I am tempted of God: for God cannot be tempted with evil, neither tempteth he any man: But every man is tempted, when he is drawn away of his own lust, and enticed. Then when lust hath conceived, it bringeth forth sin: and sin, when it is finished, bringeth forth death.
(James 1:13-15 KJV)

Only by knowing God's Word and how it is applied in life can we understand how to resist the devil (then he will flee).

Biblical Psychology

Anxious II: Intervention in Anxiety States

The first step in this intervention is to choose to correct the previous choices and decisions. Regardless of the method (mind, body, spirit) by which anxiety issues entered the life of the suffering person, intervention must start with recognizing that you can choose not be anxious. If anxiety has become neural-biological and the individual cannot focus on the counselor, then medication can be helpful (but is never a cure and should be avoided).

> *Note*: Anti-anxiety medications, known as anxioletics, are known to be some of the most addictive doctor-prescribed medications. Addiction may occur after two or three days of use. Some anxiety issues have been treated successfully with some forms of anti-depressants, which are not addictive and safer (yet, must be used with caution).

Mental Interventions

The starting point of mental interventions involves recognizing that we can choose not be anxious:

Be anxious for nothing, but in everything by prayer and supplication, with thanksgiving, let your requests be made known to God; and the peace of God, which surpasses all understanding, will guard your hearts and minds through Christ Jesus.
(Philippians 4:6-7 NKJV)

Thou wilt keep him in perfect peace, whose mind is stayed on thee: because he trusteth in thee.
(Isaiah 26:3 KJV)

We have been given the pathway to be free of anxious thoughts by placing our troubles into the hands of Jesus Christ.

We must examine the accuracy of our thoughts using the Word of God as our standard. By making sure that our thoughts line up with the Word we are able to discern inappropriate thinking.

We are destroying speculations and every lofty thing raised up against the knowledge of God, and we are taking every thought captive to the obedience of Christ,
(2 Corinthians 10:5 NASB)

Because anxiety issues represent patterns of thought that are often repetitive, the mind can become locked into loops of repeated inaccurate thought. We must change the patterns of thinking by renewing of our mind:

And be not conformed to this world: but be ye transformed by the renewing of your mind, that ye may prove what is that good, and acceptable, and perfect, will of God.
(Romans 12:2 KJV)

It is not God's will that any of us should be suffering with the anxiety of an out of control mind. He has given us the direction and power in Jesus' Name to be free.

Putting your body back on track

Because so much of the anxious experience is bodily in nature, anxiety is mental and physical, it is important to be physically healthy.

- Put structure and discipline back into your bodily health (eat, sleep, exercise).
- Practice relaxation behaviors and techniques. Choose to stop the overly busy lifestyle.
- Recognize that the anxious bodily experiences are a response to the maladaptive anxious thinking.

Spiritual changes

Adopt the spirit of humility and repentance to counteract the lies of satan. True peace will come when we make the decision to turn all of the areas of our lives over to God. When we choose not to turn things over we are really saying that we know better than God. It is simply sin in our lives. We must say NO to satan and sin by choosing the path that is Godly.

> *For the grace of God that bringeth salvation hath appeared to all men, Teaching us that, denying ungodliness and worldly lusts, we should live soberly, righteously, and godly, in this present world.*
> (Titus 2:11-12 KJV)

Choosing the spiritual path and live and think correctly:

> *This I say then, Walk in the Spirit, and ye shall not fulfill the lust of the flesh.* (Galatians 5:16 KJV)

> *Finally, brethren, whatsoever things are true, whatsoever things are honest, whatsoever things are just, whatsoever things are pure, whatsoever things are lovely, whatsoever things are of good report; if there be any virtue, and if there be any praise, think on these things.* (Philippians 4:8 KJV)

Repent and be free in Christ Jesus our Lord:

> *Repent ye therefore, and be converted, that your sins may be blotted out, when the times of refreshing shall come from the presence of the Lord.*
> (Acts 3:19 KJV)

> *'Even now,' declares the LORD, 'return to me with all your heart, with fasting and weeping and mourning. 'Rend your heart and not your garments. Return to the LORD your God, for he is gracious and compassionate, slow to anger and abounding in love, and he relents from sending calamity.'* (Joel 2:12-13 NIV)

The individual who is suffering from persistent anxious states must develop and deepen their relationship with God. Simply knowing the Creator gives peace and stops anxiety. We need a discerning spirit that can only come from knowing God.

> *The fear of the LORD is the beginning of wisdom, and the knowledge of the holy is understanding.*
> (Proverbs 9:10 KJV)
> See also John 10:4-10 and Hebrews 5:14

There must be a return to fellowship and accountability or a first time development of this practice:

> *Two are better than one; because they have a good reward for their labor.*
> (Ecclesiastes 4:9 KJV)

> *Iron sharpeneth iron; so a man sharpeneth the countenance of his friend.* (Proverbs 27:17 KJV)

When Anxiety Is Positive?

God disciplines those He loves. The world often condemns the Christian for the anxiety and guilt they experience in the course of their rebellion against the Lord. Secular psychology seeks to elevate the sin to positive attributes while condemning the response of the conscience. We should not actively alleviate anxiety rooted in stubborn, persistent, unrepentant sin. An individual in a discipling or Biblical counseling position needs to recognize God disciplines to purify us and strengthen our faith for His glory. We must leave His work alone:

Before I was afflicted I went astray, but now have I kept thy word. Thou art good and doest good; teach me thy statutes.
(Psalm 119:67-68 KJV)
See also Psalm 119:71, 75-76 & Hebrews 12:5-11.

Preventing Anxiety

In the Bible God says that we are to cast all of our care upon Him (I Peter 5:7). Our God is faithful and cares about every need (Matthew 6:25), in fact there is no problem that we face that is too difficult for our God to handle (Jeremiah 32:17, 26-17). When we face trials, we need to remember that God is sovereign and some good will manifest in the end for those who love Him and are called according to His purposes. Having an active genuine relationship with Jesus Christ provides the strength and protection that renders anxiety a waste of time and energy (Psalm 91:1-2; Phil. 4:6-7).

We are not to face difficulties in isolation, but are to remain in the fellowship of believers. This is to provide relationships of accountability, teaching on contemporary sin issues and the ministry of the Holy Spirit.

Godly balance requires wisdom which we can seek from the Lord and ask for it when we pray recognizing His system of priorities: (1) God first; (2) spouse second; (3) family third; (4) body of believers fourth; (5) job fifth. This order of priorities offers protection from the harmful effects of the world upon us. Physical balance that avoids being overworked (for the love of money), gluttony and fatigue (lack of sleep) keeps our body ready for service. Praise, prayer and fellowship develop humility that provides spiritual strength that we must have to remain healthy.

Addictive States of Mind

All addictions are <u>behavioral choices</u> that result in psychological, physiological or spiritual dependence on mood-altering substances or experiences. The Bible says that we are not to become addicted to wine (Titus 2:3), nor are we to give in to the love of money (Heb. 13:5). We are to be content with what we have. It is frequently the lack of contentment that leads to an addictive state of mind.

All things are lawful unto me, but all things are not expedient: all things are lawful for me, but I will not be brought under the power of <u>any</u>. (1 Corinthians 6:12 KJV)

All addictions are initiated with a choice. In clear-cut cases, such as illicit drugs and pornography, we see that the person chose rebellion and disobedience for the joy of a feeling. They stepped out of the will of the Father and became involved with sin that is addictive in nature. In the case of medically-prescribed medications (less clear cut), a Godly Christian who believes that they are simply following the advice of a doctor, may find him or herself psychologically and/or physiologically addicted to a medication. Their points of decision occur, first, when they are told to take the medication and fail to ask questions about potential problems, and second, when they notice they are addicted, and choose not to seek help.

The addictions that form as a result of the mood-altering behavioral practices are often hidden in the dark and may quickly become demonically involved. They can include thrill seeking, lust for money, pornography, masturbation and television shows, to name a few. In common with all of the above practices is a significant release of endorphin neurotransmitters resulting in a pleasurable high that is repeatedly sought. It is important to remember that addictions are slavery to something other than Jesus Christ, and therefore idolatry.

There are individuals who develop a dependence upon people or demons. They choose to make a person or an experience with a demon or demonic experience the sought after prize in their life. Those who become involved in satanic rituals will crave the high of the ritual experience. The devil wants them to enjoy their journey to hell. Some individuals develop a dependence on specific other persons, and feel depressed when they are not present. The mood altering experience is the absence of anxiety or depression.

Cycles

The cycle that commonly occurs in addiction is the use of the pleasurable stimulus followed by guilt over its use. The guilt is followed by sadness and depression until the pleasurable stimulus is re-experienced in order to stop the pain. It is a process that can result in such desperation that depression and/or suicide are common. God can stop any cycle if we choose to stop. The addicted individual must make the decision to stop and get help. As with much of our Christian walk, we cannot do it alone.

God Can Heal All Addictions

Recovery from addictions requires honesty about the addictive state, a desire to leave the sinful condition and repentance. God can heal the lust for the addictive element instantly, but often without confession and accountability, the addicted dog—we will return to its vomit (2 Peter 2:21-22).

For those who find themselves addicted and are unsure of how they got there, they must not look for a patsy on whom to excuse their condition. For those who have clearly chosen addiction, they must just as clearly acknowledge the error of their ways. God will not throw away the dope. The addict must take action.

Because the dominating component of addiction is the loss of control over one's behavior, it places the individual at high risk for demonic involvement.

Prayers that denounce the addiction and eliminate demons and demonic activity should be done in all cases of addiction. This is important because in the addicted mood-altered state, we are not in full control of our faculties, thus providing a door for satan to enter the individual's life.

Purely Christian Ten and Twelve step groups that acknowledge Jesus Christ as the only higher power can be an option for the individual who has been in a long-standing addictive process. We must keep in mind that our sin nature is the addiction that we are born with. Each one of us, with the power of the Holy Spirit is able to choose to stand vigilant against all sin.

In helping the addicted person:

- Pray with them for deliverance and freedom.
- Assess dangerous physiological addictive process. *(Alcohol, barbiturates, amphetamines, opiates and numerous other drugs and narcotics can develop physiological tolerance that may require medical intervention for safe withdrawal. Medical help may be needed to avoid stroke, seizures or death.)*
- Set up a system of accountability to prevent relapse.
- Help the person discover how and why they chose the addiction.
- Help them to learn through God's Word how to once again enjoy life free.

In Sum:

Addictions are a result of being mastered by something other than Jesus Christ. There is freedom from the bondage of addiction with application of God's Word and power of the Holy Spirit. Helping ourselves or others rid our lives of addictions requires love and perseverance. Often the individual feels that release from addiction in not possible, but all things are possible with God.

Appendix A
Intimacy Intervention for Marriage Relationships

Intimacy is a word that can have various definitions. Frequently, people believe that the term refers to sexual/physical contact. Although this may be a part of intimacy, it is more of a result of the presence of true intimacy rather than an expression of its true meaning.

For our purposes in this text we will define the term intimacy as the relational state existing between two individuals (for this topic, a husband and wife), wherein the relationship is personified by a truth in which each individual can say what is needed or desire to be said to the other without fear that they will be rejected. The actions that stem from this truth may take on many forms. For example, "I love you." Response: "I love you." "You hurt me." Response: "I'm sorry."

In I Corinthians 13 attitudes and functional behaviors of love are expressed and defined. We learn that love is patient, kind. It has an attitude of serving rather than demanding to be served. One of the more prominent features of that passage is found in the fact that love does not keep a record of wrongs. Many of today's marriages attempt to function under the justice principle. The justice principle states that the love I give you must be equal (equity principle) to the love you give me, and conversely, "the hurt you inflict upon me must be balanced by the hurt that I inflict upon you." This system of justice and equity is flawed at its core. Love that demands justice and a balancing of acts is fake love that keeps records of wrongs.

The keeping of a tally of wrongs is necessary only if the individual has the false belief that for them to feel okay about themselves the equity principle must be observed. This is in stark opposition to the service principle of love in marriage, serving one another in love is a command that is presented to us and nowhere in the Bible can one find the phrase "tit for tat" and "what is good for the goose is good for the gander," or vice-versa. These are borne out of the need to feel superior and the corresponding rejection of vulnerability. The truth is we are most vulnerable when we love the most. This is expressed the clearest in John 3:16: "For God so loved that He gave...," and the Jesus He gave came to serve—not to be served. Therefore the cornerstone of our love for one another is the giving of sacrificial service without the need of reciprocity or equity.

Marriages that are in advanced states of decomposition have developed rather brutal methods of establishing equity and superiority. Statements like "You always...," "You never...", and "It'll always be this way" demonstrate the impact in a relationship of keeping a record of wrongs. Once the choice has been made to keep the record, it becomes a brutal anchor that must be dragged behind to be used as a heap upon the scale of justice when one is wronged. The pattern of interaction excludes any hope of intimacy. To say something is to risk an equity attack and injury to the pride.

> *Intimacy - the relational state existing between two individuals, a husband and wife, wherein the relationship is personified by a truth in which each individual can say what is needed or desire to be said to the other without fear that they will be rejected.*

There will be mistakes in marriage. Each person will commit their share of blunders. Some of them may become repeated patterns. Some of them may be viewed as proof of the failure of an individual. In order to reestablish intimacy and deepen the form of love in a strained marital relationship, both parties must agree in prayer and principle to release and reject all records of wrong (forgiveness). The mistakes that are made in the marriage must never become part of the equalitative balance of justice. They are never to have more meaning than that of a mistake. The Bible proclaims that we have all sinned and fallen short... This is true in marriage as well as in our relationship with God. To reestablish intimacy it must be understood that walking the road of life together as a married couple carries with it that potential for one to step on the foot of the other which is ever present. Whenever the behavior of one individual results in a negative emotional experience (anger, sadness, hurt...), the correct expression of the discomfort is "ouch." The correct response to the proclamation of discomfort is "oops." The two words of "ouch" and "oops" are the simplest form of an intimacy interaction. A more precise form of intimate language would be "I feel hurt when you talk to me that way," and the only viable response is "I'm sorry. I did not mean to hurt you."

Adding to the words expletives, amplifiers and modifiers such as "You idiot! You always say stupid things to hurt me" shows retaliation and an attempt to attack with pain and a plea to balance the scales of justice. A common response that makes equal use out of records of wrongs would be a response that sounds like: "you never understand what I'm saying. You are the one who is an idiot."

Getting couples to begin to use the simple "ouch" and "oops" (related phrases), prevents the development of the record of wrongs. To set the stage for success, the counselor should insist that the couple spend 15 minutes listening to the Bible, either on tape, CD or MP3, followed by a brief time of prayer where each one prays blessings upon the other, and then the practicing of the intimacy exercise wherein the woman (who goes first) will say

"I felt _____ when you said or did _____."

This is done, based upon things that have occurred in the past 24 hours that had not been discussed up to this time. The only response that her husband may give her is:

"I'm sorry; I did not mean to cause you to feel _____."

Nothing more can be added. No embellishments are allowed in the exchange. The couple is to take turns so the man will go next by saying: "I felt _____ when you said or did _____." And she responds: "I'm sorry; I did not intend to cause you to feel _____."

There can be no discussion of the issue that has been brought up for at least 24 hours. This is to allow the individual who created the "ouch," or the oops person, to think through their intent and methods and to consider whether or not they truly need any further discussion.

The exercise <u>must be performed daily</u>, following the Scripture reading and prayer, and optimally at the same time each day, in a quiet atmosphere with no interruptions from children, cell phones or pets. The goal that will be achieved after a few weeks of faithful practice is the extinguishing of the equity principle and replacing it with intimacy based upon the giving of loving service. The 24 hours of thinking about the errors that one has committed results in the ability to take those thoughts captive so the errors are not repeated. The result of openly accepting the anger, hurt and frustration from another as a result of an action is trust, confidence and peace. This form of intimacy is the foundation of our relationship with Christ Who accepts us as we are and loves us in response to all of our hurt and anger. Couples who refuse to practice the exercise, love the power of their records of wrong and can go no further until they repent of their rebellion against an all-loving God.

Being in a Righteous Condition

The Bible tells us that our righteousness is as filthy rags. We have no ability to be righteous on our own. So what is Biblical righteousness? Because we all sin and fall short of the glory of God, then if follows that to be in right standing with God involves something other than our efforts to be sinless.

The KEY:

1 John 1:9 If we confess our sins, he is faithful and just to forgive us our sins and to cleanse us from all unrighteousness.

Therefore: To be righteous is to be cleansed from our sin after we confess. Not just a confession, but a turning away. God knows our heart and fake confessions do not fly!

God is not listening by Dr. John Gill (1690-1771)
John 9:31 - *Now we know that God heareth not sinners*,.... All mankind are sinners, even God's elect; yea, such who are truly gracious and righteous persons; for there is no man without sin; and God hears such who cry unto him day and night; such Christ came to save; for such he died; and these he calls to repentance; and every penitent sinner God hears: but by "sinners" are meant notorious sinners, such in whom sin reigns, who live in sin, and particularly impostors. The man takes up the word the Jews had made use of, and applied to Christ (John 9:24), and suggests, that had Jesus been a sinner, that is, an impostor, God would not have heard him, or have assisted him in doing a miracle, to support an imposture, or cover and encourage a fraud; but that he was heard and assisted, was a plain case: whereas not only they, the learned doctors of the nation, but such an illiterate man as himself knew, that notoriously wicked men, cheats, and deceivers, were not heard of God; and this was known from the Scripture, and all experience; see Psalm 66:18.

Sin in the heart by Adam Clark (1715-1832)
Psalm 66:18 - *If I regard iniquity in my heart* - "If I have seen (ראיתי raithi) iniquity in my heart," if I have known it was there, and encouraged it; if I pretended to be what I was not; if I loved iniquity, while I professed to pray and be sorry for my sin; the Lord, אדני Adonai, my Prop, Stay, and Supporter, would not have heard, and I should have been left without help or support.

> **James 5:16** *Confess your faults to one another, and pray for one another, that ye may be healed. The effectual fervent prayer of a righteous man availeth much.*

> *A man and woman who are Righteous before the Living God are those that obey His Commands in their marriage.*

Why this diversion in the discussion of couples intimacy? Praying for one another when in a Biblical righteous condition has great power and effectiveness. Our relationship with God sets the tone for our relationship with each other. 1Peter 3:7 tells men that they are to be understanding and honor their wives or their prayers will be hindered. If they are unrepentant they have no power in their prayers. If they sin against their wives and disobey God they are spiritually weak. If women are disrespectful to their husbands they have no prayer life of any account no matter how long they spend in the prayer closet. Unrepentant sin destroys prayer effectiveness.

Appendix B:

Scripture References for Marriage/Family and Church Relationships

Marriage and Family Relationships

EPH 5:22 Wives, submit yourselves unto your own husbands, as unto the Lord. **23** For the husband is the head of the wife, even as Christ is the head of the church: and he is the saviour of the body. **24** Therefore as the church is subject unto Christ, so *let* the wives *be* to their own husbands in every thing.

EPH 5:25 Husbands, love your wives, even as Christ also loved the church, and gave himself for it; **26** That he might sanctify and cleanse it with the washing of water by the word, **27** That he might present it to himself a glorious church, not having spot, or wrinkle, or any such thing; but that it should be holy and without blemish. **28** So ought men to love their wives as their own bodies. He that loveth his wife loveth himself. **29** For no man ever yet hated his own flesh; but nourisheth and cherisheth it, even as the Lord the church: **30** For we are members of his body, of his flesh, and of his bones. **31** For this cause shall a man leave his father and mother, and shall be joined unto his wife, and they two shall be one flesh. **32** This is a great mystery: but I speak concerning Christ and the church. **33** Nevertheless let every one of you in particular so love his wife even as himself; and the wife *see* that she reverence *her* husband.

EPH 6:1 Children, obey your parents in the Lord: for this is right. **2** Honour thy father and mother; (which is the first commandment with promise;) **3** That it may be well with thee, and thou mayest live long on the earth.

EPH 6:4 And, ye fathers, provoke not your children to wrath: but bring them up in the nurture and admonition of the Lord.

1CO 7:12 But to the rest speak I, not the Lord: If any brother hath a wife that believeth not, and she be pleased to dwell with him, let him not put her away. **13** And the woman which hath an husband that believeth not, and if he be pleased to dwell with her, let her not leave him. **14** For the unbelieving husband is sanctified by the wife, and the unbelieving wife is sanctified by the husband: else were your children unclean; but now are they holy.

1CO 7:15 But if the unbelieving depart, let him depart. A brother or a sister is not under bondage in such *cases*: but God hath called us to peace. **16** For what knowest thou, O wife, whether thou shalt save *thy* husband? or how knowest thou, O man, whether thou shalt save *thy* wife?

MT 19:8 He saith unto them, Moses because of the hardness of your hearts suffered you to put away your wives: but from the beginning it was not so. **9** And I say unto you, Whosoever shall put away his wife, except *it be* for fornication, and shall marry another, committeth adultery: and whoso marrieth her which is put away doth commit adultery.

MT 5:31 It hath been said, Whosoever shall put away his wife, let him give her a writing of divorcement: **32** But I say unto you, That whosoever shall put away his wife, saving for the cause of fornication, causeth her to commit adultery: and whosoever shall marry her that is divorced committeth adultery.

1CO 7:1 Now concerning the things whereof ye wrote unto me: *It is* good for a man not to touch a woman. **2** Nevertheless, *to avoid* fornication, let every man have his own wife, and let every woman have her own husband. **3** Let the husband render unto the wife due benevolence: and likewise also the wife unto the husband. **4** The wife hath not power of her own body, but the husband: and likewise also the husband hath not power of his own body, but the wife. **5** Defraud ye not one the other, except *it be* with consent for a time, that ye may give yourselves to fasting and prayer; and come together again, that Satan tempt you not for your incontinency. **6** But I speak this by permission, *and* not of commandment. **7** For I would that all men were even as I myself. But every man hath his proper gift of God, one after this manner, and another after that.

GAL 5:16 This I say then, Walk in the Spirit, and ye shall not fulfil the lust of the flesh. **17** For the flesh lusteth against the Spirit, and the Spirit against the flesh: and these are contrary the one to the other: so that ye cannot do the things that ye would. **18** But if ye be led of the Spirit, ye are not under the law.

GAL 5:19 Now the works of the flesh are manifest, which are *these*; Adultery, fornication, uncleanness, lasciviousness,

GAL 5:22 But the fruit of the Spirit is love, joy, peace, longsuffering, gentleness, goodness, faith, **23** Meekness, temperance: against such there is no law. **24** And they that are Christ's have crucified the flesh with the affections and lusts. **25** If we live in the Spirit, let us also walk in the Spirit. **26** Let us not be desirous of vain glory, provoking one another, envying one another.

COL 3:12 Put on therefore, as the elect of God, holy and beloved, bowels of mercies, kindness, humbleness of mind, meekness, longsuffering; **13** Forbearing one another, and forgiving one another, if any man have a quarrel against any: even as Christ forgave you, so also *do* ye. **14** And above all these things *put on* charity, which is the bond of perfectness.

HEB 13:4 Marriage *is* honourable in all, and the bed undefiled: but whoremongers and adulterers God will judge. **5** *Let your* conversation *be* without covetousness; *and be* content with such things as ye have: for he hath said, I will never leave thee, nor forsake thee. **6** So that we may boldly say, The Lord *is* my helper, and I will not fear what man shall do unto me.

Warnings to the Church Regarding Evil Behaviors

1TI 6:3 If any man teach otherwise, and consent not to wholesome words, *even* the words of our Lord Jesus Christ, and to the doctrine which is according to godliness; **4** He is proud, knowing nothing, but doting about questions and strifes of words, whereof cometh envy, strife, railings, evil surmisings, **5** Perverse disputings of men of corrupt minds, and destitute of the truth, supposing that gain is godliness: from such withdraw thyself.

RO 1:18 For the wrath of God is revealed from heaven against all ungodliness and unrighteousness of men, who hold the truth in unrighteousness;
19 Because that which may be known of God is manifest in them; for God hath shewed *it* unto them. **20** For the invisible things of him from the creation of the world are clearly seen, being understood by the things that are made, *even* his eternal power and Godhead; so that they are without excuse:

RO 1:21 Because that, when they knew God, they glorified *him* not as God, neither were thankful; but became vain in their imaginations, and their foolish heart was darkened. **22** Professing themselves to be wise, they became fools, **23** And changed the glory of the uncorruptible God into an image made like to corruptible man, and to birds, and fourfooted beasts, and creeping things.

RO 1:24 Wherefore God also gave them up to uncleanness through the lusts of their own hearts, to dishonour their own bodies between themselves: **25** Who changed the truth of God into a lie, and worshipped and served the creature more than the Creator, who is blessed for ever. Amen.

RO 1:26 For this cause God gave them up unto vile affections: for even their women did change the natural use into that which is against nature: **27** And likewise also the men, leaving the natural use of the woman, burned in their lust one toward another; men with men working that which is unseemly, and receiving in themselves that recompence of their error which was meet.

RO 1:28 And even as they did not like to retain God in *their* knowledge, God gave them over to a reprobate mind, to do those things which are not convenient; **29** Being filled with all unrighteousness, fornication, wickedness, covetousness, maliciousness; full of envy, murder, debate, deceit, malignity; whisperers, **30** Backbiters, haters of God, despiteful, proud, boasters, inventors of evil things, disobedient to parents, **31** Without understanding, covenantbreakers, without natural affection, implacable, unmerciful: **32** Who knowing the judgment of God, that they which commit such things are worthy of death, not only do the same, but have pleasure in them that do them.

Church Leadership

1TI 3:1 This *is* a true saying, If a man desire the office of a bishop, he desireth a good work. **2** A bishop then must be blameless, the husband of one wife, vigilant, sober, of good behaviour, given to hospitality, apt to teach; **3** Not given to wine, no striker, not greedy of filthy lucre; but patient, not a brawler, not covetous; **4** One that ruleth well his own house, having his children in subjection with all gravity; **5** (For if a man know not how to rule his own house, how shall he take care of the church of God?) **6** Not a novice, lest being lifted up with pride he fall into the condemnation of the devil. **7** Moreover he must have a good report of them which are without; lest he fall into reproach and the snare of the devil.

1TI 3:8 Likewise *must* the deacons *be* grave, not doubletongued, not given to much wine, not greedy of filthy lucre; **9** Holding the mystery of the faith in a pure conscience. **10** And let these also first be proved; then let them use the office of a deacon, being *found* blameless.

1TI 3:11 Even so *must their* wives *be* grave, not slanderers, sober, faithful in all things.

1TI 3:12 Let the deacons be the husbands of one wife, ruling their children and their own houses well. **13** For they that have used the office of a deacon well purchase to themselves a good degree, and great boldness in the faith which is in Christ Jesus.

TIT 1:5 For this cause left I thee in Crete, that thou shouldest set in order the things that are wanting, and ordain elders in every city, as I had appointed thee: **6** If any be blameless, the husband of one wife, having faithful children not accused of riot or unruly. **7** For a bishop must be blameless, as the steward of God; not selfwilled, not soon angry, not given to wine, no striker, not given to filthy lucre; **8** But a lover of hospitality, a lover of good men, sober, just, holy, temperate; **9** Holding fast the faithful word as he hath been taught, that he may be able by sound doctrine both to exhort and to convince the gainsayers.

Appendix C
Scriptures on the Heart from Proverbs.

Proverbs on the Heart:

PR 1:23 Turn you at my reproof: behold, I will pour out my spirit (heart) unto you, I will make known my words unto you.

PR 2:2 So that thou incline thine ear unto wisdom, *and* apply thine heart to understanding;

PR 2:10 When wisdom entereth into thine heart, and knowledge is pleasant unto thy soul;

PR 3:1 My son, forget not my law; but let thine heart keep my commandments:

PR 3:3 Let not mercy and truth forsake thee: bind them about thy neck; write them upon the table of thine heart:

PR 3:5 Trust in the LORD with all thine heart; and lean not unto thine own understanding.

PR 4:4 He taught me also, and said unto me, Let thine heart retain my words: keep my commandments, and live.

PR 4:21 Let them not depart from thine eyes; keep them in the midst of thine heart.

PR 4:23 Keep thy heart with all diligence; for out of it *are* the issues of life.

PR 5:12 And say, How have I hated instruction, and my heart despised reproof;

PR 6:14 Frowardness *is* in his heart, he deviseth mischief continually; he soweth discord.

PR 6:18 An heart that deviseth wicked imaginations, feet that be swift in running to mischief,

PR 6:21 Bind them continually upon thine heart, *and* tie them about thy neck.

PR 6:25 Lust not after her beauty in thine heart; neither let her take thee with her eyelids.

PR 7:3 Bind them upon thy fingers, write them upon the table of thine heart.

PR 7:25 Let not thine heart decline to her ways, go not astray in her paths.

PR 10:8 The wise in heart will receive commandments: but a prating fool shall fall.

PR 10:20 The tongue of the just *is as* choice silver: the heart of the wicked *is* little worth.

PR 11:20 They that are of a froward heart *are* abomination to the LORD: but *such as are* upright in *their* way *are* his delight.

PR 12:23 A prudent man concealeth knowledge: but the heart of fools proclaimeth foolishness.

PR 12:25 Heaviness in the heart of man maketh it stoop: but a good word maketh it glad.

PR 13:12 Hope deferred maketh the heart sick: but *when* the desire cometh, *it is* a tree of life.

PR 14:10 The heart knoweth his own bitterness; and a stranger doth not intermeddle with his joy.

PR 14:13 Even in laughter the heart is sorrowful; and the end of that mirth *is* heaviness.

PR 14:30 A sound heart *is* the life of the flesh: but envy the rottenness of the bones.

PR 14:33 Wisdom resteth in the heart of him that hath understanding: but *that which is* in the midst of fools is made known.

PR 15:13 A merry heart maketh a cheerful countenance: but by sorrow of the heart the spirit is broken.

PR 15:14 The heart of him that hath understanding seeketh knowledge: but the mouth of fools feedeth on foolishness.

PR 15:15 All the days of the afflicted *are* evil: but he that is of a merry heart *hath* a continual feast.

PR 15:28 The heart of the righteous studieth to answer: but the mouth of the wicked poureth out evil things.

PR 15:30 The light of the eyes rejoiceth the heart: *and* a good report maketh the bones fat.

PR 16:1 The preparations of the heart in man, and the answer of the tongue, *is* from the LORD.

PR 16:5 Every one *that is* proud in heart *is* an abomination to the LORD: *though* hand *join* in hand, he shall not be unpunished.

PR 16:9 A man's heart deviseth his way: but the LORD directeth his steps.

PR 16:21 The wise in heart shall be called prudent: and the sweetness of the lips increaseth learning.

PR 16: The heart of the wise teacheth his mouth, and addeth learning to his lips.

PR 17:3 The fining pot *is* for silver, and the furnace for gold: but the LORD trieth the hearts.

PR 17:20 He that hath a froward heart findeth no good: and he that hath a perverse tongue falleth into mischief.

PR 17:22 A merry heart doeth good *like* a medicine: but a broken spirit drieth the bones.

PR 18:12 Before destruction the heart of man is haughty, and before honour *is* humility.

PR 18:15 The heart of the prudent getteth knowledge; and the ear of the wise seeketh knowledge.

PR 19:3 The foolishness of man perverteth his way: and his heart fretteth against the LORD.

PR 19:21 *There are* many devices in a man's heart; nevertheless the counsel of the LORD, that shall stand.

PR 20:5 Counsel in the heart of man *is like* deep water; but a man of understanding will draw it out.

PR 20:9 Who can say, I have made my heart clean, I am pure from my sin?

PR 21:1 The king's heart *is* in the hand of the LORD, *as* the rivers of water: he turneth it whithersoever he will.

PR 21:2 Every way of a man *is* right in his own eyes: but the LORD pondereth the hearts.

PR 21:4 An high look, and a proud heart, *and* the plowing of the wicked, *is* sin.

PR 22:11 He that loveth pureness of heart, *for* the grace of his lips the king *shall be* his friend.

PR 22:15 Foolishness *is* bound in the heart of a child; *but* the rod of correction shall drive it far from him.

PR 22:17 Bow down thine ear, and hear the words of the wise, and apply thine heart unto my knowledge.

PR 22:18 For *it is* a pleasant thing if thou keep them within thee; they shall withal be fitted in thy lips.

PR 23: For as he thinketh in his heart, so *is* he: Eat and drink, saith he to thee; but his heart *is* not with thee.

PR 23:12 Apply thine heart unto instruction, and thine ears to the words of knowledge.

PR 23:15 My son, if thine heart be wise, my heart shall rejoice, even mine.

PR 23:17 Let not thine heart envy sinners: but *be thou* in the fear of the LORD all the day long.

PR 23:19 Hear thou, my son, and be wise, and guide thine heart in the way.

PR 23:26 My son, give me thine heart, and let thine eyes observe my ways.

PR 24:12 If thou sayest, Behold, we knew it not; doth not he that pondereth the heart consider *it*? and he that keepeth thy soul, doth *not* he know *it*? and shall *not* he render to *every* man according to his works?

PR 24:17 Rejoice not when thine enemy falleth, and let not thine heart be glad when he stumbleth:

PR 24:32 Then I saw, *and* considered (applied my heart) *it* well: I looked upon *it, and* received instruction.

PR 25:20 *As* he that taketh away a garment in cold weather, *and as* vinegar upon nitre, so *is* he that singeth songs to an heavy heart.

PR 26:23 Burning lips and a wicked heart *are like* a potsherd covered with silver dross.

PR 26:24 He that hateth dissembleth with his lips, and layeth up deceit within him (in his heart);

PR 26:25 When he speaketh fair, believe him not: for *there are* seven abominations in his heart.

PR 27:9 Ointment and perfume rejoice the heart: so *doth* the sweetness of a man's friend by hearty counsel.

PR 27:11 My son, be wise, and make my heart glad, that I may answer him that reproacheth me.

PR 27:19 As in water face *answereth* to face, so the heart of man to man.

PR 28:14 Happy *is* the man that feareth alway: but he that hardeneth his heart shall fall into mischief.

Appendix D

Scriptures on the Heart from Psalms

Heart in the Psalms:

PS 4:7 Thou hast put gladness in my heart, more than in the time *that* their corn and their wine increased.

PS 5:9 For *there is* no faithfulness in their mouth; their inward part (heart) *is* very wickedness; their throat *is* an open sepulchre; they flatter with their tongue.

PS 7:10 My defence *is* of God, which saveth the upright in heart.

PS 9:1 I will praise thee, O LORD, with my whole heart; I will shew forth all thy marvellous works.

PS 10:3 For the wicked boasteth of his heart's desire, and blesseth the covetous, *whom* the LORD abhorreth.

PS 11:2 For, lo, the wicked bend *their* bow, they make ready their arrow upon the string, that they may privily shoot at the upright in heart.

PS 13:2 How long shall I take counsel in my soul, *having* sorrow in my heart daily? how long shall mine enemy be exalted over me?

PS 13:5 But I have trusted in thy mercy; my heart shall rejoice in thy salvation.

PS 14:1 The fool hath said in his heart, *There is* no God. They are corrupt, they have done abominable works, *there is* none that doeth good.

PS 15:2 He that walketh uprightly, and worketh righteousness, and speaketh the truth in his heart.

PS 16:7 I will bless the LORD, who hath given me counsel: my reins (heart) also instruct me in the night seasons.

PS 16:9 Therefore my heart is glad, and my glory rejoiceth: my flesh also shall rest in hope.

PS 17:3 Thou hast proved mine heart; thou hast visited *me* in the night; thou hast tried me, *and* shalt find nothing; I am purposed *that* my mouth shall not transgress.

PS 18:45 The strangers shall fade away (lose heart), and be afraid out of their close places.

PS 19:8 The statutes of the LORD *are* right, rejoicing the heart: the commandment of the LORD *is* pure, enlightening the eyes.

PS 19:14 Let the words of my mouth, and the meditation of my heart, be acceptable in thy sight, O LORD, my strength, and my redeemer.

PS 20:4 Grant thee according to thine own heart, and fulfil all thy counsel.

PS 21:2 Thou hast given him his heart's desire, and hast not withholden the request of his lips. Selah.

PS 22:14 I am poured out like water, and all my bones are out of joint: my heart is like wax; it is melted in the midst of my bowels.

PS 24:4 He that hath clean hands, and a pure heart; who hath not lifted up his soul unto vanity, nor sworn deceitfully.

PS 25:17 The troubles of my heart are enlarged: *O* bring thou me out of my distresses.

PS 26:2 Examine me, O LORD, and prove me; try my reins and my heart.

PS 27:3 Though an host should encamp against me, my heart shall not fear: though war should rise against me, in this *will* I *be* confident.

PS 27:8 *When thou saidst*, Seek ye my face; my heart said unto thee, Thy face, LORD, will I seek.

PS 27:14 Wait on the LORD: be of good courage, and he shall strengthen thine heart: wait, I say, on the LORD.

PS 28:7 The LORD *is* my strength and my shield; my heart trusted in him, and I am helped: therefore my heart greatly rejoiceth; and with my song will I praise him.

PS 30:12 To the end that *my* glory (heart) may sing praise to thee, and not be silent. O LORD my God, I will give thanks unto thee for ever.

PS 31:24 Be of good courage, and he shall strengthen your heart, all ye that hope in the LORD.

PS 32:11 Be glad in the LORD, and rejoice, ye righteous: and shout for joy, all *ye that are* upright in heart.

PS 33:11 The counsel of the LORD standeth for ever, the thoughts of his heart to all generations.

PS 36:1 The transgression of the wicked saith within my heart, *that there is* no fear of God before his eyes.

PS 36:10 O continue thy lovingkindness unto them that know thee; and thy righteousness to the upright in heart.

PS 37:4 Delight thyself also in the LORD; and he shall give thee the desires of thine heart.

PS 37:31 The law of his God *is* in his heart; none of his steps shall slide.

PS 38:8 I am feeble and sore broken: I have roared by reason of the disquietness of my heart.

PS 38:10 *My heart pounds, my strength fails me; even the light has gone from my eyes.*

PS 39:3 My heart was hot within me, while I was musing the fire burned: *then* spake I with my tongue,

PS 40:8 I delight to do thy will, O my God: yea, thy law *is* within my heart.

PS 40:10 I have not hid thy righteousness within my heart; I have declared thy faithfulness and thy salvation: I have not concealed thy lovingkindness and thy truth from the great congregation.

PS 40:12 For innumerable evils have compassed me about: mine iniquities have taken hold upon me, so that I am not able to look up; they are more than the hairs of mine head: therefore my heart faileth me.

PS 41:6 And if he come to see *me*, he speaketh vanity: his heart gathereth iniquity to itself; *when* he goeth abroad, he telleth *it*.

PS 44:21 Shall not God search this out? for he knoweth the secrets of the heart.

PS 45:1 My heart is inditing a good matter: I speak of the things which I have made touching the king: my tongue *is* the pen of a ready writer.

PS 49:3 My mouth shall speak of wisdom; and the meditation of my heart *shall be* of understanding.

PS 51:10 Create in me a clean heart, O God; and renew a right spirit within me.

PS 51:17 The sacrifices of God *are* a broken spirit: a broken and a contrite heart, O God, thou wilt not despise.

PS 53:1 The fool hath said in his heart, *There is* no God. Corrupt are they, and have done abominable iniquity: *there is* none that doeth good.

PS 55:4 My heart is sore pained within me: and the terrors of death are fallen upon me.

PS 55:21 *The words* of his mouth were smoother than butter, but war *was* in his heart: his words were softer than oil, yet *were* they drawn swords.

PS 57:7 My heart is fixed, O God, my heart is fixed: I will sing and give praise.

PS 58:2 Yea, in heart ye work wickedness; ye weigh the violence of your hands in the earth.

PS 61:2 From the end of the earth will I cry unto thee, when my heart is overwhelmed: lead me to the rock *that* is higher than I.

PS 62:10 Trust not in oppression, and become not vain in robbery: if riches increase, set not your heart *upon them*.

PS 64:6 They search out iniquities; they accomplish a diligent search: both the inward *thought* of every one *of them*, and the heart, *is* deep.

PS 64:10 The righteous shall be glad in the LORD, and shall trust in him; and all the upright in heart shall glory.

PS 66:18 If I regard iniquity in my heart, the Lord will not hear *me*:

PS 69:20 Reproach hath broken my heart; and I am full of heaviness: and I looked *for some* to take pity, but *there was* none; and for comforters, but I found none.

PS 73:1 Truly God *is* good to Israel, *even* to such as are of a clean heart.

PS 73:13 Verily I have cleansed my heart *in* vain, and washed my hands in innocency.

PS 73:21 Thus my heart was grieved, and I was pricked in my reins.

PS 73:26 My flesh and my heart faileth: *but* God *is* the strength of my heart, and my portion for ever.

PS 77:6 I call to remembrance my song in the night: I commune with mine own heart: and my spirit made diligent search.

PS 78:72 So he fed them according to the integrity of his heart; and guided them by the skilfulness of his hands.

PS 84:2 My soul longeth, yea, even fainteth for the courts of the LORD: my heart and my flesh crieth out for the living God.

PS 86:11 Teach me thy way, O LORD; I will walk in thy truth: unite my heart to fear thy name.

PS 86:12 I will praise thee, O Lord my God, with all my heart: and I will glorify thy name for evermore.

PS 89:50 Remember, Lord, the reproach of thy servants; *how* I do bear in my bosom (heart) *the reproach of* all the mighty people;

PS 90:12 So teach *us* to number our days, that we may apply *our* hearts unto wisdom.

PS 94:15 But judgment shall return unto righteousness: and all the upright in heart shall follow it.

PS 97:11 Light is sown for the righteous, and gladness for the upright in heart.

PS 101:2 I will behave myself wisely in a perfect way. O when wilt thou come unto me? I will walk within my house with a perfect heart.

PS 101:4 A froward heart shall depart from me: I will not know a wicked *person*.

PS 101:5 Whoso privily slandereth his neighbour, him will I cut off: him that hath an high look and a proud heart will not I suffer.

PS 102:4 My heart is smitten, and withered like grass; so that I forget to eat my bread.

PS 104:15 And wine *that* maketh glad the heart of man, *and* oil to make *his* face to shine, and bread *which* strengtheneth man's heart.

PS 108:1 O God, my heart is fixed; I will sing and give praise, even with my glory.

PS 109:22 For I *am* poor and needy, and my heart is wounded within me.

PS 111:1 Praise ye the LORD. I will praise the LORD with *my* whole heart, in the assembly of the upright, and *in* the congregation.

PS 112:7 He shall not be afraid of evil tidings: his heart is fixed, trusting in the LORD. **8** His heart *is* established, he shall not be afraid, until he see *his desire* upon his enemies.

PS 119:2 Blessed *are* they that keep his testimonies, *and that* seek him with the whole heart.

PS 119:7 I will praise thee with uprightness of heart, when I shall have learned thy righteous judgments.

PS 119:10 With my whole heart have I sought thee: O let me not wander from thy commandments.

PS 119:11 Thy word have I hid in mine heart, that I might not sin against thee.

PS 119:30 I have chosen the way of truth: thy judgments have I laid *before me (*in my heart*)*.

PS 119:32 I will run the way of thy commandments, when thou shalt enlarge my heart.

PS 119:34 Give me understanding, and I shall keep thy law; yea, I shall observe it with *my* whole heart.

PS 119:36 Incline my heart unto thy testimonies, and not to covetousness.

PS 119:58 I intreated thy favour with *my* whole heart: be merciful unto me according to thy word.

PS 119:69 The proud have forged a lie against me: *but* I will keep thy precepts with *my* whole heart.

PS 119:80 Let my heart be sound in thy statutes; that I be not ashamed.

PS 119:111 Thy testimonies have I taken as an heritage for ever: for they *are* the rejoicing of my heart.

PS 119:112 I have inclined mine heart to perform thy statutes alway, *even unto* the end.

PS 119:145 I cried with *my* whole heart; hear me, O LORD: I will keep thy statutes.

PS 119:161 Princes have persecuted me without a cause: but my heart standeth in awe of thy word.

PS 125:4 Do good, O LORD, unto *those that be* good, and *to them that are* upright in their hearts.

PS 131:1 LORD, my heart is not haughty, nor mine eyes lofty: neither do I exercise myself in great matters, or in things too high for me.

PS 138:1 I will praise thee with my whole heart: before the gods will I sing praise unto thee.

PS 139:23 Search me, O God, and know my heart: try me, and know my thoughts:

PS 141:4 Incline not my heart to *any* evil thing, to practise wicked works with men that work iniquity: and let me not eat of their dainties.

PS 143:4 Therefore is my spirit overwhelmed within me; my heart within me is desolate.

PS 148:14 He also exalteth the horn of his people, the praise of all his saints; *even* of the children of Israel, a people near unto him (to his heart). Praise ye the LORD.

Appendix E
Scripture verses on Freedom

PS 119:45 And I will walk at liberty: for I seek thy precepts.

ISA 61:1 The Spirit of the Lord GOD *is* upon me; because the LORD hath anointed me to preach good tidings unto the meek; he hath sent me to bind up the brokenhearted, to proclaim liberty to the captives, and the opening of the prison to *them that are* bound;

JER 34:8 *This is* the word that came unto Jeremiah from the LORD, after that the king Zedekiah had made a covenant with all the people which *were* at Jerusalem, to proclaim liberty unto them;

JER 34:17 Therefore thus saith the LORD; Ye have not hearkened unto me, in proclaiming liberty, every one to his brother, and every man to his neighbour: behold, I proclaim a liberty for you, saith the LORD, to the sword, to the pestilence, and to the famine; and I will make you to be removed into all the kingdoms of the earth.

RO 8:18 For I reckon that the sufferings of this present time *are* not worthy *to be compared* with the glory which shall be revealed in us. **19** For the earnest expectation of the creature waiteth for the manifestation of the sons of God. **20** For the creature was made subject to vanity, not willingly, but by reason of him who hath subjected *the same* in hope, **21** Because the creature itself also shall be delivered from the bondage of corruption into the glorious liberty of the children of God.

1CO 8:9 But take heed lest by any means this liberty of yours become a stumblingblock to them that are weak.

1CO 10:27 If any of them that believe not bid you *to a feast*, and ye be disposed to go; whatsoever is set before you, eat, asking no question for conscience sake. **28** But if any man say unto you, This is offered in sacrifice unto idols, eat not for his sake that shewed it, and for conscience sake: for the earth *is* the Lord's, and the fulness thereof: **29** Conscience, I say, not thine own, but of the other: for why is my liberty judged of another *man's* conscience? **30** For if I by grace be a partaker, why am I evil spoken of for that for which I give thanks?

2CO 3:17 Now the Lord is that Spirit: and where the Spirit of the Lord *is*, there *is* liberty. **18** But we all, with open face beholding as in a glass the glory of the Lord, are changed into the same image from glory to glory, *even* as by the Spirit of the Lord.

GAL 2:4 And that because of false brethren unawares brought in, who came in privily to spy out our liberty which we have in Christ Jesus, that they might bring us into bondage: **5** To whom we gave place by subjection, no, not for an hour; that the truth of the gospel might continue with you.

GAL 5:1 Stand fast therefore in the liberty wherewith Christ hath made us free, and be not entangled again with the yoke of bondage.

GAL 5:13 For, brethren, ye have been called unto liberty; only *use* not liberty for an occasion to the flesh, but by love serve one another.

JAS 1:25 But whoso looketh into the perfect law of liberty, and continueth *therein*, he being not a forgetful hearer, but a doer of the work, this man shall be blessed in his deed.

JAS 2:12 So speak ye, and so do, as they that shall be judged by the law of liberty. **13** For he shall have judgment without mercy, that hath shewed no mercy; and mercy rejoiceth against judgment.

1PE 2:16 As free, and not using *your* liberty for a cloke of maliciousness, but as the servants of God. **17** Honour all *men*. Love the brotherhood. Fear God. Honour the king.

1PE 2:19-20 While they promise them liberty, they themselves are the servants of corruption: for of whom a man is overcome, of the same is he brought in bondage. **20** For if after they have escaped the pollutions of the world through the knowledge of the Lord and Saviour Jesus Christ, they are again entangled therein, and overcome, the latter end is worse with them than the beginning.

www.ingramcontent.com/pod-product-compliance
Lightning Source LLC
Chambersburg PA
CBHW080552170426
43195CB00016B/2761